Speak Easy

by **Sandy Linver**

as told to Loral Dean

SUMMIT BOOKS

NEW YORK LONDON TORONTO SYDNEY TOKYO

Summit Books
Simon & Schuster Building
Rockefeller Center
1230 Avenue of the Americas
New York, New York 10020

SUMMIT BOOKS and colophon are trademarks
of Simon & Schuster Inc.
Designed by Stanley S. Drate/Folio Graphics Co., Inc.
Manufactured in the United States of America

10 9 8 7 6 5 4 3 2 1 Pbk.

Library of Congress Cataloging in Publication Data
Linver, Sandy.
  Speak easy.

  1. Public speaking.   I. Title.
PN4121.L54   808.5'1   78-10612
ISBN: 0-671-67224-X Pbk.

Permission to reprint the following is gratefully acknowledged:
  From *The People, Yes* by Carl Sandburg, copyright 1936 by Harcourt
Brace Jovanovich, Inc.; copyright © 1964 by Carl Sandburg. Reprinted by
permission of the publishers.

For my mother, my brother and Buddy—with love.
For my wonderful father, who knew what it meant to
reach out.

Contents

Foreword

Sandy Linver should not have written this book. She should have met with you in the quiet of your office or your home so that the two of you could discuss her simple, straightforward ideas about effective speaking and how they apply to you.

But that would be the best of all possible worlds. This book cannot substitute for personal instruction from Sandy, but it will help you take an honest look at yourself and the way you communicate. And it will show you how to become the best speaker you can be.

More than thirty years ago, a Jesuit priest who served as my debate coach in college said that something happens to the human animal when he moves from a sitting to a standing position. A person who possesses the God-given ability to talk, unique to the human animal, and is normally articulate, becomes something less than human when he finds himself in front of an audience of more than two people. Something happens to the link between mind and speech, and for some reason he believes he has to project something other than what he really is.

I have had the privilege of seeing Sandy work with a number of executives over a period of years. She has a remarkable ability to show people how to be naturally themselves when they find themselves in front of a collection of other human beings.

As you read her ideas about spoken communication, paragraph by paragraph, chapter by chapter, you will find nothing very startling. Like most good teachers, Sandy uses straightforward language, and her premise is easy to understand. But the ideas in this book should be of enormous help to you in learning to express the best of what you are.

If you bought this book, you were wise. If someone gave it to you, you were lucky!

DONALD R. KEOUGH
President
The Coca-Cola Company

Your Spoken Image:
A Personal Evaluation

The purpose of this book is to help you improve your spoken image. To do so, it is important that you take time to thoughtfully answer the following questions *before reading the book*.

1. List the qualities you think an effective speaker should have.
2. Which of these qualities do you now have?
3. List your speaking strengths.
4. List your speaking weaknesses.
5. Do you think you can overcome your speaking weaknesses? If so, how?
6. In what situations do you have the most difficulty speaking with others? Why?
7. Do you have any "hangups" that adversely affect the way you speak? If so, what are they and why do you think you have them? Do you think they can be overcome? If so, how?
8. What kind of initial impression do you leave with oth-

ers? List adjectives to describe the way they see you (physical appearance, dress, facial expression, the way you move). List adjectives to describe the way they hear you (sound of your voice, the way you express yourself).

9. How would you like people to see you? How would you like people to hear you?

1

Your Spoken Image

When people ask me what I do, I don't say I'm a speech coach, a public-speaking teacher, or a speech consultant. I say I help people improve their spoken image.

Before I discuss what I mean by a person's *"spoken image,"* let's consider the word *image* in its broader sense. *Image,* according to one dictionary definition, means "the concept of someone held by the public or the character projected by someone to the public." Very simply, then, our image is the way other people perceive us.

Our image depends to a certain extent on the labels others attach to us because of our occupation, income level, marital status, age, color, nationality, religious beliefs, and so on. We cannot control the preconceived image other people have of us based on those labels, but when we meet another person, we immediately project an additional impression—our visual image. We exercise a great deal of control over this image because it is determined by much more than the physical features we were born with. It is determined by the way we dress, move, groom ourselves and style our hair, by our weight, our physical condition, our posture and our facial expressions.

We think of the image-conscious person as the meticulous groomer, the person in designer clothes or wearing the latest fad. But whether or not we think of ourselves as image-conscious, with all the advertising hype that implies, we all make conscious choices about the way we present ourselves to the world. "Not caring" what we wear, or choosing clothes for comfort rather than style, are also image-conscious choices. We are simply choosing a different image.

The choices we make about our visual image determine to a great extent how other people perceive us—until we open our mouths and speak. At that moment, many of us destroy our carefully constructed facades, because few of us are as completely in control of our spoken image as we are of our visual image. The minute we begin to speak, our spoken image becomes dominant and overrides our visual image and all our other images based on job, age, sex, color, class and nationality.

Our spoken image consists of much more than the words we say. It's how we say the words, the sound of our voice, the way we use our body as we speak—all of which determine how effectively we convey our message.

The way we interact with other people—both personally and professionally—has very little to do with the written word. It is almost totally based on speaking. Yet most people rarely consider how important the way they speak is to every aspect of their relationships with other people. They invest years of training, education, work, energy and emotion in their work and their personal relationships, but never invest any time at all in improving their spoken image.

Both our success in our work and our personal happiness

depend a great deal on our speaking abilities. Sure, education, writing ability, job performance and personality are important, too. But what happens when we talk to people exerts such a powerful influence that it can destroy—or reinforce—all our other positive attributes and achievements.

The president of an executive search company telephoned me because she had heard I was familiar with a certain public relations firm. She was trying to decide whether to retain the firm. "I've seen their portfolio and I can see they've been involved in some innovative projects," she said. "But quite frankly I didn't think the person who came to talk to me could sell anything." That company lost a contract because its representative was not in control of his spoken image.

No matter what your occupation, your success depends a lot on the effectiveness of your spoken image. People choose a doctor, lawyer or dentist on the basis not only of his professional reputation but also the way he relates to them personally. A salesperson, stock broker, real estate agent, restaurateur—anyone who deals with the public—has to establish rapport with his clients, and that rapport is established verbally. Even in jobs that do not involve interaction with people on a day-to-day basis, a person's speaking skills often are crucial to getting the job and keeping it.

And occupations traditionally considered number- or paper-oriented are becoming more people-oriented today. Public demand has forced many businesses to become more aware of the services they offer. For example, banks have drastically expanded their range of services to customers. Such services as interest-bearing checking accounts and home equity loans show a new awareness that serving people is the key to survival in the highly competitive banking environment. Certified public accountants, once stereotyped in the public mind as recluses in green eyeshades sitting on high stools adding up columns of numbers, now find clients demanding that they relate to them as human beings. And television is so pervasive that industries, businesses, public figures and even private individuals once insulated from public scrutiny often find themselves literally on camera, whether they choose to be or not.

One-to-One Versus Public Speaking

We all speak every day, naturally, without rehearsal and without notes. We rarely give our speaking abilities a second thought—until we're asked to give a speech. Then it's a different story. Immediately we get tense and nervous about having to stand up and perform in front of an audience. We worry about forgetting what we have planned to say, about stumbling over our words, about our voice cracking, that our audience will think us inarticulate, bumbling or incompetent.

Although most people never stop to analyze the way they speak until they are in the spotlight in front of an audience, I believe we should be just as concerned about how well we speak in our everyday conversations. Every time we open our mouths we deliver a speech of sorts, and our spoken image depends much more on our everyday speaking style than it does on the occasional speech we deliver. And my experience helping hundreds of clients to improve their public speaking skills has demonstrated that people usually demonstrate the same weaknesses in one-to-one conversation as they do when speaking to a group.

Everyday speaking cannot be considered separately from public speaking because effective speaking anywhere and anytime means being in full control of what you are saying and how you say it, understanding the way your audience is receiving your message (*audience* throughout this book will refer to the recipient of a message, whether it be one person or many), knowing how to use your voice and how to use pause, and understanding the entire scope of the speaking situation. Your personality, attitude toward other people, control over your spoken image, and ability to apply basic speaking principles are equally important in all speaking situations. This book will help you develop a speaking style that should be effective on the telephone, across your desk, or when you are talking to a friend, a colleague, a small group or an auditorium filled with people.

The Best of You

A shy, timid woman once asked me if she should develop a special public-speaking image that she could turn on every time she gave a speech. Her question brought up an important point: Can developing a more effective spoken image mean developing a new identity? Might you have to change who and what you are in order to become a more effective speaker? I don't think so. Let me illustrate with Michael's story.

An engineer working for a large computer company, Michael came to me for help when he was promoted to marketing director. After twenty years working alone at a desk, he had to sell his expertise to other people. He was a controlled, reticent, self-conscious person who felt that selling somehow diminished his status as a professional. And he felt uncomfortable and inadequate trying to establish personal rapport with customers and employees.

The first time he gave a speech to the class, he explained what he had done for the past twenty years. His job was highly technical and difficult to explain in layman's terms. He did try to explain it in simplified language, but he gave the class no more reason to listen than if he'd said, "This is what I've done to earn a living for the past two decades and I'm going to tell you about it." He stood stiffly; his hands never moved from his sides; he avoided eye contact with the group; and he spoke in a matter-of-fact, flat voice.

When he finished, I asked him if he found his work interesting or stimulating in any way. "Of course," he replied. "If I didn't, I wouldn't have stayed with it all these years." "Then why didn't you let your audience know that?" I asked.

Michael had been schooled in Europe in the forties in an upper-class, rigidly disciplined boys' school, where memorizing facts was considered much more important than any kind of creativity. He had been taught that gentlemen never gesture or display any emotions when they speak.

I often ask students to role-play—impersonate a character totally different from their own—to help them get outside themselves and shake ingrained body and speech patterns. I told Michael to impersonate an aggressive salesman. He pretended he was a street-corner flower vendor, a role he found very silly. I videotaped his presentation and played it back with the sound turned off. He was amazed at how sincere and authoritative he looked—not at all like the silly, unsophisticated character he thought he had been playing.

When he began to loosen up a little in his serious talks, Michael was amazed at the genuine interest he could spark in an audience, about a field he had always dismissed as obscure to the average person. For the first time, he was able to bring to the surface the enthusiasm and fascination for his profession he had always felt inside. He had avoided people all his life, not because he was a misanthrope, but because he had never learned how to relax with anything except a book. Once convinced that it wasn't really low-class or ill-bred to speak with the vitality and enthusiasm I call *energy*, much of his discomfort in dealing with people face-to-face evaporated. In his new position as marketing director he found he didn't need to change his personality to be successful; he simply had to develop areas of his personality that in the past had been suppressed.

As Michael's experience illustrates, developing a more effective spoken image does not mean developing a special public-speaking personality that you turn on every time you give a speech, nor does it mean transforming yourself into a different person. I don't believe in pouring people into molds they don't fit or trying to turn them into something they're not.

You simply have to learn to project the person you really are or, as I phrase it to my students, "become the best of you." Becoming the best of you may mean developing speaking strengths that have been hidden or suppressed within you for various reasons. But it doesn't mean developing a phony speaking personality.

People often ask me for a list of good speakers so that they can emulate them. I always ask these people whom *they* consider good speakers. I believe there are no right or wrong ways to speak; what matters is the speaker's effectiveness—his ability to get his message across to his audience. If the audience hears, understands and responds to a speech, it doesn't matter how the speaker did it or how much traditional speech etiquette he ignores. What matters is that he's effective.

This book neither follows an academic method nor encourages you to adopt a "Speakeasy method" or a "Speakeasy style." It shows you how to develop a personal speaking style that works for you. It doesn't matter how you do it, as long as it's effective—as long as you make something happen.

The effective speaker is not necessarily polished and perfect. He is energetic, involved and willing to be a direct, open human being. And the same principles apply whether he's talking to his closest friend or to an audience of five hundred.

2

E.A.S.Y.

I chose the name "Speakeasy" for my firm because it describes simply and concisely the way I believe speaking should be. The Speakeasy approach makes speaking easy in any situation—whether you are speaking to a friend, a business associate, or an auditorium filled with people. It is my philosophy of communication, developed through working with hundreds of people involved in all kinds of jobs. Most of them have made dramatic improvements in their speaking skills. It can work for you too.

The Speakeasy approach revolves around four basic concepts. As you read this book you will find that everything I say relates to at least one of them. The four concepts are *Energy*, *Awareness*, *Strength* (or Self-Esteem) and *You*. Together, the first letters spell EASY—the way speaking should and can be.

Energy

To make an audience listen, a speaker must have energy. Energy and power are closely related. Energy usually refers to power in action or, as one dictionary phrases it, "power exercised with vigor and determination," "vitality," or "intensity of expression."

The energy necessary for effective speaking can best be defined as intensity or involvement. It is the force that impels a speaker to reach out to make contact with an audience. I have been asked if my concept of energy means enthusiasm. It can be enthusiasm; but it isn't necessarily that, because energy doesn't have to be happy.

You must feel and experience energy to really understand what it is. I believe there is energy at the core of everyone. It is what enables us to survive. In a primitive society, people use most of their energy to satisfy their basic needs of food, clothing and shelter. In our highly developed society, people utilize their energy to meet more complex needs, such as respect, recognition and emotional, intellectual or spiritual fulfillment.

Energy in a businessperson is the drive to meet whatever challenges are necessary to attain a goal. The energy may be generated by a desire for money, power or fame or by an urge to compete. But no matter what its source, energy is the drive that enables him to reach his goal.

To be successful in any endeavor, you must be able to tap your energy when you need it. Shortly before the last national election, one of my students—a politician—spoke at a breakfast meeting. There was nothing wrong with the content of his speech, but his delivery was lifeless. If I'd had to decide whether to vote for or against him on the basis of that speech alone, I definitely would have voted against him. When the speech was over, I told him what I thought. "Oh," he said

offhandedly, "I was tired. I'm not good early in the morning."
"You were tired, were you?" I said, astonished at his casual
attitude. "Well, that's really tough. If you're going to win this
race, you'll have to wake up and care about your audience no
matter what time of day it is."

If an audience is important enough to speak to, you have an
obligation to find the energy you need to reach out—no matter
how tired you may be at that particular moment. On some days
I teach two seminars—one lasting all day and the other for three
hours in the evening—and I feel drained at five P.M. But when
I walk into the classroom at six o'clock and see a new, expectant
group of people, my feelings of responsibility toward that audience overcome my lack of energy. I will the energy to come,
because I know it's up to me to make something happen.

Think for a moment about the people you enjoy listening to.
I'm sure you'll agree that they all have energy. Energy doesn't
have to be loud. It can be a quiet intensity generated across a
desk. Using energy in a quiet conversation, or when speaking
to a thousand people in a convention hall, simply means saying
everything as if you mean it. The difference between the two
situations is in the amount of vocal projection required, not in
the energy level.

I believe we all begin our lives with equal energy potential.
Think of it as a reservoir of water with a network of channels
leading from it. How much water we use depends on the number of channels that become blocked. Energy blocks are our
inhibitions, some of them healthy and necessary to survival
within our culture, and some destructive. A woman may block
her business energy because she believes her maternal energy
should be dominant; or she may suppress her competitive energy because she believes it to be incompatible with femininity. A child's musical energy might be blocked because his
parents consider playing an instrument a waste of time. A
man's creative energy might be blocked by utilitarian family

values that dismiss writers, sculptors or painters as unproductive; his entrepreneurial energy might be suppressed by an environment that stresses the importance of financial security.

There are many potential blocks to a speaker's energy. A speaker's body energy may be blocked by a speech teacher who says that ladies should stand with one foot centered in front of the other or that gentlemen should never gesture with their hands. A woman's vocal energy may be blocked if she believes that raising her voice will make her sound masculine, harsh or aggressive. But the most common block to a speaker's energy is the desire to deliver a perfect, polished speech. When a speaker tries to be perfect, his energy is turned inward and transmuted into tension. Instead of directing his energy outward toward the audience, he worries about the specific words he will say, how they will sound, and whether they will come out exactly as he planned them.

The president of a large retail chain attended one of my seminars. He was articulate, his speeches were well organized, and he was a warm, likable person. But he was so boring he consistently lost his audience within two minutes of beginning his speech. His problem was lack of energy.

By the second day of the seminar, he was beginning to let go and put some energy into his speeches. When he watched himself on videotape, he agreed it looked good and was effective. "But," he said, "it feels strange to me. Am I not being phony?"

It's not phony to find a new energy level if it makes you a more effective speaker. Look at it the way you would any new situation in which you feel strange or uncomfortable. Holding a tennis racket or golf club for the first time feels unnatural, but after you've practiced holding it and worked at using it, it becomes comfortable. If a stiff, controlled person recognizes that his formality and reserve have been choking channels of communication with other people and decides that having an audience listen and respond is worth the risk of reaching out more, I don't believe he's being phony. Changing ingrained habits is risky because it means abandoning comfortable patterns, but it doesn't mean becoming a different person. It *can* mean uncovering a self that has been hidden or suppressed, sometimes for a person's entire lifetime.

In my experience, few people are really tuned in to their energy level when they speak. Many people think that raising their voice or gesturing even slightly will make them appear overbearing, aggressive or silly. To show them they are wrong, I put students through the exercise described in the last chapter, in which they assume a personality totally different from their own to deliver a speech. Sometimes I suggest a personality with characteristics the student has a deficiency in, such as authoritativeness, assertiveness, physical demonstrativeness or enthusiasm, and other times I tell them to act out a comical or silly role.

I've had Abraham Lincolns, Ralph Naders, Bella Abzugs, W. C. Fieldses, religious fanatics, waitresses, taxi drivers, hookers and door-to-door salesmen portrayed in these classes. The results often are surprising. When I play back a videotape with the sound turned off, the students' body images usually are not the silly, aggressive or overbearing ones expected. As Michael, the European-born engineer, recognized, the body image usually is close to that of a relaxed, authoritative—and energetic—person.

A speaker's energy level affects much of what he does with his voice, face and body. Many people ask me for exercises to improve the quality of their voices or specific tips on how to stand or use their hands. I can teach formal exercises in articulation, breathing and inflection if a student really needs coaching in a specific area. But more often people need to tune in to their energy level rather than brush up on specific skills. Once they understand their energy level, such problems as stiff body movements or too soft a voice usually correct themselves.

All this relates to my whole approach to speaking. Pointers, rules and how-to's rarely help the whole person; understanding my concept of energy and how it affects what people do with their voices and bodies will do much more to improve a person's speaking effectiveness. Many speech teachers emphasize phony eye contact or a fixed, pleasant smile, or give specific hints on how to gesture to emphasize a point. I say, "There's someone you need to reach out to. Look at him." Or, "Relax and enjoy it and let the smile happen." Or, "Let go and let your hands and feet do what they have to do."

That's energy.

Letting your energy out doesn't mean being unduly emotional or "letting it all hang out." Your energy level must be appropriate; if it is too high, you bludgeon your audience with your energy instead of reaching out to them. If you are so intent on saying something that you become arrogant, loud or aggressive, you are no more effective than the person with too little energy—because you are totally unaware of your audience.

Awareness

Brian, a handsome, six-foot, thirty-five-year-old plastics manufacturer, announced with an expansive smile at the beginning of one of my seminars that he was an "SOB—the son of the boss." His father was a very different person from himself, Brian went on. He thought communications seminars and the like were a waste of time. He didn't care about people the way Brian did; he just wanted to run the business and make a profit.

This wasn't the first self-improvement course Brian had taken. He had come to my seminar, he said, because he cared a lot about people, and learning to relate to people better would help him communicate how much he cared.

When Brian gave a speech, he turned on a pleasant smile and spoke with a strong voice and lots of enthusiasm. There was nothing wrong with his energy level. But he didn't really speak to the people in the group. He performed. None of his talk of caring about people carried through in his actions. Although there were only ten persons in the seminar, he never really saw anyone; he consistently lost track of how long he had been speaking; and he muddied the main points of his speeches with long, irrelevant tangents.

When I talked with the group about the importance of learning how to listen, Brian said it was just what he needed. But ten minutes later, when members of the group were giving speeches, he was busy writing instead of listening. When it was his turn to talk, I pretended not to listen. I looked around the room at everything and everyone except him, then started to write in my notebook. It was a few minutes before he noticed. When he finally did, he stopped speaking.

"How does it feel?" I asked. Embarrassed, he laughed nervously and said, "I see what you mean. I'm so interested in what I'm saying that I just assume everyone else will be, too."

The speaker must remember that speaking should always be a two-way process. It means not only making contact with an audience but getting feedback from them as well. And that's impossible if the speaker lacks the sensitivity that I call "audience awareness."

Many people—particularly business persons—place too much emphasis on the content of a speech. They organize their material carefully and stand up to speak with the attitude that the information they are about to convey is important enough to guarantee the audience's attention. They're enthusiastic and send out plenty of energy. But they are oblivious to the way their audience receives their information.

The speaker—not the speech—determines how the message is received. If he is not super-sensitive to the way his audience responds, his energy may be wasted.

In later chapters I will give specific tips on how to develop audience awareness, but the basis of audience awareness is genuinely caring what the audience thinks. If you care, you will learn to listen to them as closely with your eyes as you expect them to listen to you with their ears. When you learn how to do this, you will quickly sense an audience's approval, disagreement or indifference, and your energy level will adjust accordingly.

Listening with your eyes is not superficially scanning a group so that everyone gets a bit of eye contact. That's meaningless, ineffectual and phony. Authentic audience awareness must come from an impulse within you to genuinely focus your attention outward and establish contact with as many human beings as possible within the room. Ideally, it means relating to each member of the audience as an individual and opening yourself up to him. It means establishing intimacy between you and your audience.

If you're too wrapped up in yourself and your message, you will never develop audience awareness. But if you stop thinking about yourself and pay attention to what is going on out there, your gut will respond to your audience. This kind of gut response means that if, after five minutes of a twenty-minute speech, you realize that your audience isn't with you, you will adapt in order to pull them back in. It may mean throwing the session open to questions; or it may mean simply abbreviating the speech and emphasizing a few key points. The specifics will fall into place—if you care. Your desire to make something happen will enable you to shift, adapt and bend, and do whatever is necessary to get involved with your audience.

When people are listening—really listening—they will look you in the eye, ask questions, smile, frown, nod their heads or raise an eyebrow. And there's a feel in the room, too. It's a "gut" feeling, and you develop a sensitivity to it by watching people very closely. But when it's there and you know it's there, it's delicious. It's contact.

Strength

I remember giving a morning seminar to thirty bright, very successful young salesmen. When I began speaking, the group was restless; four individuals were particularly disruptive. One was reading a newspaper; two others were talking; another was noisily shifting in his chair. I didn't take the disruptions personally, because the group didn't know me, and I was quite willing to bend and adapt. But I made up my mind immediately that I would not put up with that kind of disrespect for the entire morning.

I put the group through a communications exercise in which groups of two talk, first sitting back to back, then facing each other with their eyes closed, then shaking hands with their eyes still closed. When they had finished, I zeroed in on the ringleader and asked him how he felt about the exercise.

He leaned back in his chair and looked around the room to be sure he had an audience. "Well," he said, slowly and deliberately, "I was a bit worried for a moment." "Why?" I asked. "You see, I didn't know whether my neighbor here was a high shaker or a low shaker," he replied. "I'm afraid I don't understand what you mean," I said evenly. "Well, you see," he said, smirking, "I didn't know how good his aim with his hand was." A hush fell over the room as the men waited to see how I would handle the situation. I paused for a moment, then looked him straight in the eye and said in a controlled voice, "Well, is his aim with his hand any better than yours is with your mouth?"

I didn't disagree with him, I didn't try to make a total fool of him, and I didn't become hysterical. I simply asked a direct question.

I heard a distinct sigh of relief from the group. They were relieved to see I was in control. The troublemaker broke the tension by smiling and then the group laughed, as if the entire incident had been just lighthearted banter. From that moment on, everyone in the group cooperated and began to participate actively in the seminar.

If you've prepared your material, if you reach out and put out energy, and if you're sensitive to your audience, you have a right to expect attention and respect from your audience whether or not they agree with your views. I was prepared to leave the salesmen's seminar if the group refused to grant me the respect and attention I deserved. The incident illustrates my third concept: the strength or the self-esteem to hold on to who and what you are. I was willing to adapt and bend if the audience genuinely needed or expected something different from me. But I was not willing to put up with rudeness, nor was I prepared to bend and adapt to the point of giving up who or what I am. That's too high a price for anyone to pay.

One of the fears speakers express most often is of the person in the audience who is obviously out to get them. The important thing to remember when someone tries to intimidate you is that he is more interested in how you handle a hostile question than he is in your specific response. In other words, your delivery is just as important as what you actually say. If someone makes a sweeping charge or asks a question that would take an hour to answer properly, the most important thing is to answer coolly and directly and not become angry, emotional or irrational. If the question or charge is impossible to answer briefly, make a general statement about your views on the subject and conclude with something like, "I think you wanted more information but our time is limited," or, "I hope that answered your question." A statement like that takes the teeth out of the opposition because it is straightforward and honest. It's difficult for someone to remain hostile if his rancor is not returned.

Strength also means not being afraid to "deal with the reality" in the audience. If you sense a disruption, go to the source of the problem—deal with the reality—instead of talking on as if you were oblivious to it. This may not be easy to do with a very large group but it usually can be done with a pause or a look. When the audience is less than, say, one hundred people, you usually can zero in and ask what's going on, if someone has a question or if someone disagrees. This means risking a confrontation, of course. That's why it requires strength.

In my discussion of audience awareness, I said your goal was to make contact with your audience. Making contact doesn't always mean establishing rapport. Not every audience is going to give you a standing ovation; simply making some audiences sit up and listen is an accomplishment. Sensitivity to your audience means caring enough to find out their feelings, ideas and reactions; it does not mean simply reinforcing their ideas. You are there to stimulate the audience and give them something new. You must have the strength to give them what you believe they need to hear—which isn't necessarily what they want to hear or something they agree with.

I recently accepted an invitation to speak about effective communication to a women's volunteer organization. The meeting was held in a long, narrow room; the group's officers were sitting in the front row and the rest of the women—about three hundred—were sitting at the back of the room. I had requested a neck microphone so that I could move freely, but arrived to find that none had been provided. So I stepped down from the stage to get closer to the group and said, "I don't have a mike so I would appreciate it if you would all move to the front."

No one moved.

I repeated my request a second time. This time three people moved. I waited a few minutes longer and then said, "Perhaps I haven't made myself clear. If you stay where you are and don't move forward, you won't be able to hear me. I know you're comfortable sitting with your friends but I believe it will be a more productive meeting for all of us if I don't have to stand up on the stage behind that lectern."

The air was charged and I could feel the hostility and resentment in the room. But after a few more minutes of silence, the women began to move forward—slowly.

I had prepared a half-hour talk on communication, but when the group finally was assembled at the front of the room I said, "I was asked to speak to you about methods of effective communication, but I'm not going to say what I had planned." I paused, looked them in the eye, and went on: "I tell my students to plan their speeches carefully but to be ready to adapt to the needs of their audience. I thought you were an organization dedicated to helping other people, to reaching out to persons in the community less fortunate than yourselves. Yet you were unable to reach out enough to *me* to get off your comfortable chairs and move a little closer so that we could make contact. If you can't move ten rows down so that we can make contact, I can't believe you really want to reach out to the people in your community." I went on to talk about my concept of "reaching out" to other people if we genuinely want to communicate with them.

I made contact with that audience and, as it happened, their hostility had changed to receptiveness by the time I finished. A number of the women came up to me afterwards, thanked me, and said it had been just what they needed to shake up their comfortable patterns of behavior.

I relate this incident to illustrate two points: First, the speaker, not the audience, should control the speaking situation. If I had begun to speak despite the fact that the women had ignored my request to move forward, I would have tacitly conceded that they were in charge of the situation, not I. Second, the speaker should consider himself a teacher as much as a lecturer; he must have the strength to tell the audience what they need to hear, rather than merely what they want or expect to hear. It takes a strong speaker to be able to risk what I did by standing my ground and refusing to speak until the group cooperated; but by doing so, and then being straight in what I said, I really communicated a message and expanded the group's awareness instead of simply massaging their egos. The speaker is not out to win friends. If his desire for audience approval is so strong that he lets the audience control him, his purpose as a speaker and teacher is lost.

Nor is the speaker there to identify with his audience. The audience wants to know where the speaker is coming from and they expect him to understand their position and to accept them. But pretending you're one of your audience when you're not—for example, a forty-year-old businessman wearing jeans and a T-shirt to give a speech to a group of college students—is one of the easiest ways to make a fool of yourself.

I remember a student practicing a speech he was going to deliver to a group of black mayors meeting in Atlanta. The speech was well-organized but it was a manuscript speech and he exerted very little energy as he read it. The class found the speech boring, so I asked them for suggestions about how to make it come alive. One student suggested, "Why don't you throw in a few *Hey, brother's* and expressions like that?"

He was making two dangerous assumptions. First, just because the audience was black, he assumed they would use expressions like "hey, brother." Second, even if they did use that kind of language, he assumed they wanted the speaker to identify with them.

Strength, or self-esteem, means having a strong, secure sense of self which you will not allow your audience to threaten. More about that in Chapter 4.

You

Ask yourself three questions. First, how much work, energy, education and training have you invested to bring yourself to the point where you are now professionally? Second, do you understand the enormous impact your spoken image has on your success? And third, how much time and effort have you invested in even thinking about your spoken image?

A stockbroker who plays a lot of tennis has attended several of my seminars. His speaking skills have improved only slightly. The reason? He is willing to attend seminars, but he is not willing to invest time and effort outside the classroom to work on his speaking skills. I have told him that if he would devote a fraction of the time he spends improving his tennis game to improving his spoken image, he would be an outstanding speaker by now.

I don't offer a magic formula for instant speaking success. Like it or not, it all comes back to you and how much time and effort you are willing to devote to improving your spoken image. You can attend dozens of communications seminars and read a stack of books on the subject, but if you don't deal with yourself and your own personal speaking strengths and weaknesses, you will have wasted your time.

How much this book helps you depends on you. If you read it in a detached way, you won't benefit much. But if you really think about how it relates to you personally, you'll get a lot out of it. My ideas are important only inasmuch as they stimulate you to reevaluate your ideas about what makes a speaker effective and how you personally can become a more effective speaker.

In Chapter 12, I describe how to stand back and objectively analyze your own individual speaking style. Once you have done this, the rest is up to you. You may discover ingrained habits and speech patterns that are ineffective. They may be as comfortable as an old shoe, but if you genuinely want to improve your spoken image, you will have to discard them. Change is never easy, and how much you improve will depend first on how willing you are to risk making changes—because change always involves risk—and then on how determined you are to do so. Becoming an effective speaker, like acquiring or improving any worthwhile skill, will require perseverance, discipline and a lot of effort.

And just as there is no magic formula for effective speaking, there is no one right way to achieve it. I do not preach a "Speakeasy Method" or a "Sandy Linver Style." It all depends on you—your individual needs, your speaking strengths and weaknesses, and the real you inside which you want to project to your audience. The right way for *you* to speak effectively will not be quite the same as the right way for anyone else.

3

The Flavor
of You

"Communication" has become a buzz word in both the business world and among the scores of self-help groups and others who offer guidance in how to enrich interpersonal relationships. Most discussions of communication point out that it is two-way: that it entails a transfer of ideas, meaning or feeling, and that it basically means a message sent out and a message received. All this is valid, but the most important element of communication is contact between two people or two groups of people.

The most authentic form of communication is physical contact. Some cultures are more physically demonstrative than others; but no matter what our cultural heritage, there are times when physical communication says things that verbal communication cannot. If you're with a friend who has been through a tragedy, you may not be able to find the right words, so you assure him of your sympathy by touching his arm, squeezing

his shoulder, or giving him a bear hug. That touch says something very basic. If a man and a woman argue and one says
"I'm sorry," it isn't quite believed until one reaches out and
takes the other's hand or touches a cheek or gives a hug. It's
easier to fake words than it is to fake physical contact, because
when we speak we reach out to another person only symbolically, with words; when we touch we reach out literally, with
our bodies.

Physical communication means less when it is an established ritual, such as shaking hands. But two people who genuinely want to make contact can impose meaning on a ritual.
You probably have experienced situations when you shook
hands perfunctorily upon meeting someone for the first time,
but when you had talked for a while and were about to part,
you reached out to shake hands again and this time it was
different. This time you were genuinely reaching out to make
contact with another human being.

I'm not saying you have to go around touching people to
communicate effectively. But I strongly believe that our feelings
about reaching out physically are closely related to how much
we are willing to reach out verbally, and in every way, to other
people.

"Reaching out," as a concept, is important to speaking, because in today's complex, highly mobile world we all have to
deal with people of different races, religions and nationalities
and with social and economic backgrounds very different from
our own. Our personal world is composed of the whole fabric
of our background: family, social and economic status, where
we have lived, interests, job and personal life. Each person's
world is unique, and for two persons to communicate there has
to be a meeting place, a common ground.

Each of us has to decide how far we are willing to reach out
of our personal world in order to find common ground with
another person. If we wait for the other person to make a move,

we may never establish contact. Reaching out of the safety and privacy of our own world involves considerable risk—risk of losing a firm foothold in our own world and risk of rejection by the person we are reaching out to. Each person has to decide how much he is willing to risk in order to establish contact with another human being. But reaching out of our personal world makes it possible for us to touch other people, physically or verbally. And touching, literally or symbolically, is communication.

When I talk to a group, regardless of size, I want to touch as many people as I can and I want as many people as possible to touch me. Touching means that I say something and the person in the fifth row smiles and nods his head or raises an eyebrow and I respond and say, "What's the matter, don't you agree with me?" and he says, "Oh, no, I was just thinking about it." And we both laugh. We've made contact.

Public speaking today is not hiding behind a lectern and being polished, perfect and detached. It's getting involved with those human beings out there. The more detached you are, the less involved you are willing to get, the less you want to get to know your audience, the less successful you're going to be as a speaker.

When I talk to a group I don't say, "Well, I've got a lot of useful information and they're going to hear it." I say, "Before I'm finished, we're going to find a place to come together; we're going to find a place for understanding—even if we don't agree. But I'm going to make something happen and I'm going to do whatever I have to do in order to make it happen."

It's this desire for contact, to make something happen, that gives a speaker energy.

Reaching out to an audience is not simply an ideal to strive for; today's audiences demand contact. Fifty years ago audiences were more content to listen to a speaker formally deliver a manuscript speech from behind a lectern. Today, television has changed all that. People who have witnessed assassinations, wars, Olympic games and political conventions live and in color are not attuned any more to the ritual of listening to a formal speech. Today's audiences are much less patient with a speaker who doesn't take the trouble to stimulate as well as inform.

Speaker, Audience and Message

Every spoken communication must balance three factors: speaker, audience and message. For effective communication to take place, each must be emphasized equally; if one is emphasized more than another, the balance is destroyed and communication suffers.

There are four basic types of speaker, each of whom balances speaker, audience and message differently.

THE APOLOGIZER

The apologizer focuses on the audience at the expense of the speaker and the message. He lacks confidence in his own worth, credibility and knowledge, so he apologizes, overexplains and repeats himself. This is the person who wastes five minutes at the beginning of a speech saying he doesn't have time to explain his ideas adequately; who tells the audience they probably know more about the subject he has been asked to speak on than he does; who instead of pausing and letting his words stand, uses fillers like "you know"; who fails to make any strong points because he gets carried away on long, irrelevant tangents or includes too many details; who so desperately wants approval from his audience that he lets them shape him and his message.

Of course this is a composite personality; a speaker who can be described as an apologizer usually exhibits only some of these characteristics. For example, I recall a president of a large multinational company giving a speech to the shareholders. He was physically a large man and was afraid his size coupled with his powerful position would intimidate people. He foolishly felt he needed to pretend to be less than he was. The words of his speech were strong, but to compensate for his size and position, he hunched his shoulders over the microphone and spoke in a very soft voice. Half the impact of his words was lost because he delivered them without any energy, and his credibility as the president of a large, dynamic company was diminished by the weak spoken image he projected.

THE PERFORMER

The performer focuses on the speaker, at the expense of the audience and the message. He impresses people at first as an accomplished speaker: He brims with self-confidence, has plenty of energy, speaks with a full, strong voice, is in command of his subject matter, seems perfectly at ease, and is the kind of person envied by others as a "natural" speaker. But as much as his audience admires his style and envies his poise, they find it hard to listen to him—although they may be hard put to say exactly why. The performer is difficult to listen to because he talks at his audience, not to them. He is so self-confident, he thinks he can tell the audience what they need to know; so he never watches for a response.

A young attorney in one of my seminars is an excellent example of the performer. He went to an Ivy League school, then spent three years as a lawyer in the army before joining a law firm. He had a precise military bearing and was the type of person who does everything well as a matter of course and expects other people to do the same. He had neither time nor patience to find out where people were; he simply put them where he thought they should be. The class's initial reaction to Derrick was unqualified admiration: "He's so bright, so articulate, so well-organized, and he never forgets." But they found themselves tuning out—although they couldn't say exactly why. The reason, of course, was that Derrick didn't really care what they thought; he talked at them instead of to them. Nor did he bother to give the audience a reason to listen. In a talk about the need for estate planning, he spoke knowledgeably and articulately. But he spoke in generalities about the law instead of relating it to the audience by telling them what it would mean to them if they were killed in an accident and their family had to cope.

THE COMPUTER

The computer focuses on the message at the expense of the audience and the speaker. He treats the speaking engagement as if there were no human beings present and delivers his message as dryly as if he were dictating a statistical report. We've all been subjected to the computer; he's the speaker responsible for the impulse to settle back in our seats and doze or daydream until a speech is over. The computer makes no attempt to impose his personality on the material or to draw the audience in. He usually reads his speech, rarely looking up to see if the audience is still there. Although he focuses on the content, he rarely gets his message across because he invests no feeling or energy and takes no notice of the audience's response. He's the student who tells me, "I agree with your approach, but of course it doesn't apply to my profession."

THE EFFECTIVE SPEAKER

The effective speaker balances self, audience and message, taking all three equally into consideration. He values himself equally with his audience; he is spontaneous and open; he prepares his material thoroughly, then speaks to the issue and responds to the audience.

E.A.S.Y.

Balancing the speaker, audience and message is really just another perspective on my E.A.S.Y. concept. To be effective, the speaker must balance his energy, audience awareness and self-esteem, and that involves equal consideration of himself, his audience and his message. The apologizer makes a pretense of audience awareness but is really just concerned with himself; because he lacks self-esteem, his energy level probably will be too low. The performer substitutes aggressiveness for the assertiveness that goes with self-esteem. His energy level is usually too high, because he lacks sensitivity to his audience. The computer's energy level is almost always too low, because he is unconcerned about projecting himself to his audience, and he will be virtually unaware of his audience's response. The effective speaker adapts his energy to a level appropriate to the audience's response, and his healthy self-esteem enables him to keep sight of his own worth while respecting that of his audience.

The Flavor of You

The most common public speaking personality in the business and professional world is the computer. Business and professional people come to me concerned about their credibility: They want to come across as serious authorities in their area of expertise. Often they tell me that my E.A.S.Y. concept may be useful for casual presentations, but *their* subjects are serious or technical and are aimed at a very specialized audience that has come to be informed rather than entertained. Their audience doesn't have to be teased, cajoled or persuaded to listen; they are there for a purpose and need only a clear, straightforward presentation of the facts.

Specialists in many fields—scientists, physicians, teachers, university professors, economists—all attend conferences with their peers. Being asked to "read a paper" at one of these gatherings is usually a coveted honor. But hearing someone read a paper is usually a mind-numbing experience. The only conceivable purpose of such gatherings is the stimulation, inspiration and motivation of face-to-face contact with persons involved in similar work. If ideas alone did that, people could mail their papers to one another.

A speaker is *never* there only to present information—no matter how technical or specialized his subject. A speech is an inefficient method of presenting very precise, detailed information, because an audience, no matter how highly trained in a specific area, can absorb a limited amount of detail by ear. If it is necessary to convey detailed or complex information, the speaker can do so much more efficiently and accurately by distributing written material for the audience to read at their leisure. Then he can present several broad ideas orally.

A speaker may think he is conveying nothing but information to his audience, but he is wrong—even if he does nothing but read a dry manuscript speech.

The reason? Your audience may or may not absorb the information you present, but like it or not, they will absorb a flavor of you. A month after your talk they probably will remember only a general idea of what you said, but they will remember you. The credibility of your information depends as much on you as on the information itself. In other words, your delivery is just as important as the actual words you say.

The actual words you use in any situation have very little to do with your credibility or the meaning you convey. "I love you" may seem like a straightforward statement, but whether it is believed or not—and what it is taken to mean—depends on the setting, the speaker's tone of voice, his facial expression, what he does with his body, the level of trust between him and his audience, and the entire context of his relationship with his audience.

A diplomat once told me that extemporaneous speeches were fine for other people, but he was required to talk about weighty subjects such as his country's foreign policy and had to read a manuscript whose exact wording had been approved by his government. I replied that he could easily distribute copies of the government's official statement to the audience and the press, but his credibility as a representative of his government was more important than simply passing on policy statements. If he knew his subject, as I assumed he did, since that was his job, he could deliver much of his speech extemporaneously and distribute the exact, government-approved words after he had finished speaking. He could read isolated sections or sentences, if they covered delicate nuances of policy that could easily be misinterpreted.

I will elaborate on the pros and cons of manuscript speeches and extemporaneous speeches in Chapter 9; my point here is that the speaker's credibility does not depend only on the words he uses; and that his job is to stimulate his audience as well as to inform them.

The rationale for giving a speech, instead of writing a report, is the physical proximity of speaker and audience, or in the case of radio or television, the visual or aural contact. A speech is a speech because there is a speaker. This is stating the obvious, but the speaker who focuses on content alone forgets or ignores this obvious fact. The speaker's prime advantage over the writer is the instantaneous response he can inspire from his audience. The speaker who is not prepared to take advantage of these powerful dynamics would communicate more effectively if he wrote instead of talked.

4

Perception and Self-Image

How You See Your Audience and Yourself

Bruce, a thirtyish pharmaceutical salesman, paid me in full weeks before an evening seminar began, because he was afraid that if he didn't, he would "chicken out." When he came with his check he impressed me with his good looks, erect posture and easygoing manner. His spoken image was consistent with his visual image. He looked me in the eye and told me in a steady voice without even a hint of a tremor that he was extremely nervous whenever he spoke and terrified when he had to give a speech. I told him he didn't appear the least bit nervous right then; he repeated that he was, even at that moment, and that he was especially tense when speaking in front of a group.

Bruce spoke to the class in exactly the same manner he had spoken with me privately—directly and with appropriate energy and eye contact. When the class told him he didn't look nervous, he repeated his story about how nervous he felt.

The second evening of the seminar he saw himself on video-tape. He was stunned. "My God!" he said, "I don't look nervous at all." "That's what we've all been trying to tell you," I said. "Well," he replied, "I really couldn't believe it until I saw it for myself."

When he watched himself on videotape the next time, Bruce grinned from ear to ear. I don't think I've ever seen a student so mesmerized with himself. He had been a good speaker from the beginning, but now he became a star performer. He spent hours preparing his talks, experimented with flip charts, gestures, styles of delivery and subjects. One week he impersonated Abraham Lincoln, complete with black suit, top hat and false beard; another, he broke up the class by striding in as one of the Wright brothers, wearing a windbreaker, cap and goggles.

Toward the end of the seminar, I was unable to keep a commitment to speak at a Cancer Society meeting and asked him to stand in for me. When he walked into class the next week, I asked him how it had gone. "Don't ask me now," he said, giving me a dark look. "I'll tell everyone in a few minutes."

When his turn to speak came, he stood up and said, "I want to tell you that this week I gave a speech for Sandy—and it wasn't good." He paused and looked dramatically around the class. "No, it wasn't good," he repeated, "it was fantastic!" Then he told us about the first speech he had ever given, when he was a teenager, to his high school assembly. His mind had gone blank and he had been laughed off the stage. The experience had been so painful he had never been able to tell anyone about it until that moment. But, he said, the seminar had caused a dramatic change in his perspective on himself and had enabled him to break through his defense mechanisms and erase the memory that had so deeply colored his perception of his speaking abilities.

The Way We See Things

Bruce had a distorted perception of his speaking ability because of a traumatic experience during his impressionable adolescent years. No matter how many people told him his self-perception was distorted, he couldn't believe it until he saw the evidence for himself. Once he saw his behavior objectively, his altered perception of himself made it possible for him to excel in an area in which he previously had always felt inadequate.

The way a speaker sees himself and his audience is infinitely more important than the so-called objective reality of the speaking situation, because how a speaker perceives himself and his audience determines in large part what happens between them. The greater the discrepancy between how the audience perceives the situation and how the speaker perceives it, the greater the problem they will have communicating with each other.

The following explanation of why we perceive the way we do should make this clear.

First, we are not born with our perceptions; our perceptions are learned through experience. There is no such thing as a "born" speaker, just as there is no such thing as a "born" athlete or musician. Experts disagree about the relative importance of heredity and environment and I don't want to enter that debate. But briefly, I believe each of us is born with many predispositions and potential talents; which ones we develop and how we develop them depend on our environment. When I was in elementary school, I enjoyed giving recitations in front of the class because the response from the teacher and the other children made me feel special. Call that a natural speaking talent if you will, but my parents noticed that I enjoyed speaking in front of a group and reinforced my "talent" by giving me elocution and drama lessons. I am not sure whether or not I was born with a flair for speaking, but I am certain that I have *learned* to speak well.

Second, each person's perception is unique and personal; no two people perceive exactly alike. Because no two persons inherit exactly the same genes or undergo exactly the same experiences, we each perceive the world around us differently. When you speak to a group you reach out from your personal world to make contact with theirs, but you can never expect to leave with them seeing everything exactly the way you do. You should try to bring them as close to your meaning as you can, but you should not have unrealistic expectations. Experience has taught me not to expect a meeting of minds every time I speak, and recognizing the limitations of human communication makes me more comfortable when my audience doesn't accept or comprehend my point of view as totally as I might like.

Third, we select what we perceive, according to our knowledge and interests. One member of an audience may not hear a word the speaker says because he is worried about catching a plane; another may not listen because she is admiring his physique and fantasizing about getting to know him; another may notice nothing but the audiovisual aids because his company manufactures a competitive product; and another may be vitally interested in the subject and listen intently to what the speaker says, but not notice what he looks like or what he is wearing. The speaker, on the other hand, can perceive his audience as a mass of hungry lions or as a group of fifty individuals, each eager to respond favorably to what he has to say. Or he may notice no one but his boss in the front row, or his parents in the back row.

Fourth, each person's perceptions are shaped by his past experiences. Bruce's perception of his speaking abilities had been shaped by his negative experience as a teenager. If a member of an audience has been bored by many speakers in the past, he probably will settle into his chair, prepared to nap or daydream throughout any speech. If a person has had positive public speaking experiences, he will approach each speech expecting to do well.

Fifth, we can alter our perceptions by undergoing new experiences. Bruce's perception of his speaking abilities changed when he saw himself objectively for the first time, without the distorting lens of his past negative experience. If you have avoided speaking in public all your life or have always been dissatisfied with your performance in front of a group, you probably perceive yourself as a poor speaker, condemned to remain so. But if you agree that we learn our perceptions, you should understand that you were not born to speak the way you do—that if you're shy, it's because you've learned to be shy, and that if you mumble or stand stiffly, you've learned that too.

The way we accumulate perceptions is comparable to the way a computer functions. A computer stores information in programs fed into it from an outside source. It can calculate, organize and draw conclusions only about information it has been programmed with; it cannot draw on any outside information.

But if the program does not contain appropriate data, it can be replaced by a new one.

Changing Your Programming

Our programming is our experience and how it has taught us to perceive. It is the sum total of our lives; it has made us what we are, and it is not easy to change. But if we stand back and analyze our programming—or at least become aware of what it is—we can work to change it, little by little.

To become an effective speaker, you may have to unlearn

negative perceptions resulting from past experiences. You will have to learn some new techniques and expose yourself to new speaking experiences to build positive perceptions of yourself as a speaker. But it is important to remember that learning to speak well in public does not involve learning an entirely new skill, as you would, for example, if you were learning to play the piano and had never played a musical instrument before. Most of us speak every day of our lives; learning to speak well in front of a group is simply learning a new facet of a skill whose basics you already have mastered. To continue the music analogy, it's like learning to play popular music when you have been trained in classical music, or learning to play the oboe when you already know how to play the clarinet.

Becoming an effective speaker is harder for some people than others because their programming has been consistently negative. It is never easy to discard or alter ingrained habits. But it is always possible when a person is motivated and willing to work at it.

The questionnaire at the end of this chapter will help you see yourself more objectively. I cannot guarantee the dramatic self-recognition that Bruce experienced, but if you take the time to really think about your perceptions and how they have been molded by your past experiences, you probably will gain some useful insights into your speaking skills. Chapter 12 gives tips on how to take an honest, objective look at your speaking skills and how to improve them.

What You See Is What You Get

Drove up a newcomer in a covered wagon: "What kind of folks live around here?" "Well, stranger, what kind of folks was there in the country you come from?" "Well, they was mostly a lowdown, lying, gossiping, backbiting lot of people." "Well, I guess, stranger, that's about the kind of folks you'll find around here." And the dusty grey stranger had just about blended into the dusty grey cottonwoods in a clump on the horizon when another newcomer drove up. "What kind of folks live around here?" "Well, stranger, what kind of folks was there in the country you come from?" "Well, they was mostly a decent, hardworking, law abiding, friendly lot of people." "Well, I guess, stranger, that's about the kind of people you'll find around here." And the second wagon moved off and blended with the dusty grey. . . .

—Carl Sandburg *

What you see in your audience is what you will get. This may sound at first like motivational hype, but I truly believe it. I believe it because perception is experience-related: Our perceptions feed on our past experiences and reinforce them. This is why the adage that success breeds success is essentially true. It's easier to get a job when you have a job because prospective employers perceive you as successful. The author of a bestseller is guaranteed an audience for his next book because readers perceived his first book favorably and hope the next will match it.

Human nature being what it is, if we send out a positive message, we more than likely will get a positive one in return; if we send out a negative one, we'll get negative feedback. Before I go in to speak to a group, I strongly believe it will be a successful encounter because I have had many successful speaking experiences in the past. This doesn't mean I psych myself into believing happy things will happen or blithely assume all speaking situations are alike. It means I trust my ability to make something successful happen because I have proven

* From *The People, Yes* (New York: Harcourt Brace and World, 1936).

to myself in the past that I can do it. If it is a difficult speaking situation, I will work to make it successful: I will use my energy, listen to my audience, and make every effort to bring us together.

The speaker who perceives himself as ill-prepared and inadequate will probably speak apologetically to his audience; they in turn will doubt his competence. The speaker who perceives his audience as hostile will probably speak aggressively and spark a hostile response. The speaker who perceives his audience as attentive and responsive will probably speak to them in a direct, straightforward manner and be received with respect and attention.

I have seen this syndrome countless times. One student was forced by his employer to deliver a speech to a group of city planners when he believed it would be more productive if they simply read a paper he had written. He felt his ideas were too complex to be presented orally and believed he couldn't possibly do it well. After he delivered the speech, he told me he had made a mess of it—just as he expected. Another time, I attended a seminar for business and the media, designed to encourage better communication between the two. A columnist from a national business publication attended because she wanted to visit Atlanta; but she believed the seminar would be a waste of time because she had attended similar ones in the past and felt she had nothing more to learn. She read a manuscript speech with very little energy, bored her audience, and no one learned much from the encounter. A young reporter from a local newspaper, excited by the possibility of impressing national newspeople, delivered a well-prepared extemporaneous speech that stimulated excellent audience response and repartee. A person in middle management gave a speech instead of his boss and apologized profusely because, he said, the audience had been expecting someone much more knowledgeable and important than he; he then spoke in a monotone with such low energy the audience quickly tuned him out. His expectations were fulfilled: He knew they didn't want to listen to him; they had come to hear his boss.

The expectations with which you approach a speech are extremely important because if you walk into a situation expecting it to be bad for you, you will tend to treat it as if it already is a failure and give up before giving it a chance. If, on the other hand, you are convinced you can have a positive experience, you will not settle for anything less.

Who Am I?

How we see our audience begins with the way we see ourselves. Every time we speak to another person or group our feelings about ourselves color our perception of the exchange between us.

"What you see is what you get" is as true about the way we see ourselves as it is about our perception of others, because we build our self-image from the feedback we receive from other people. Our self-image is determined by our answers to three questions:

> Who am I?
> How am I doing? and
> How am I doing compared to others?

We answer all three questions on the basis of feedback from other people. Our initial feedback came from our parents or the persons who reared us. If we were constantly criticized for our failings and inadequacies, we probably developed a negative self-image. If we were encouraged to do our best and praised for our accomplishments, and at the same time loved unconditionally so that we knew we were "OK" no matter what we did, we received a solid base on which to build a positive self-image.

Because communication is always two-way, we begin to influence the kind of feedback we receive at a very early age. If we're told we're clumsy, we feel clumsy and act clumsy; if we're told we dance gracefully, we'll probably continue to dance and become even more graceful. If we develop a negative self-image at an early age, it begins a vicious circle that can be very hard to break. Bruce developed a negative image of himself as a public speaker when he was a teenager, because of the derisive feedback he received from his high school audience, and could not shake it for years afterwards.

Being Authentic with Your Audience

The question you have to ask yourself is: If I feel inadequate, insecure or apologetic whenever I stand up to speak in front of a group, is it just nervousness based on a normal kind of tension, experienced by almost everyone who performs in public, or is it related to something more basic about my image of myself? The effective speaker must consider himself a winner. If he doesn't, he will communicate his feelings of inadequacy to his audience, and they will doubt his authority and question his credibility.

Many professionals and technically oriented people confuse the kind of assertiveness necessary for effective speaking with the crass image of the hale-fellow-well-met salesman. Keith, a psychologist in one of my classes, was very sensitive to his audience but spoke very softly and completely suppressed his energy. His father had been the stereotypical salesman and Keith had grown up constantly embarrassed by his loud, brash manner. As a result, he overcompensated.

Considering yourself a winner doesn't mean you have to develop a super-inflated ego and project the obnoxious salesman image that Keith deplored. On the contrary, it means having the honesty and courage to be authentic with your audience and project to them who you really are.

The stronger and more secure your self-image, the more authentically you will project yourself in every speaking situation. This means not being afraid to be honest about your abilities and accomplishments. If you're an expert in aerodynamics or computers or management training, your audience has a right to know that. You owe them the courtesy of informing them that their time isn't going to be wasted listening to a rookie. If you're not a *bona fide* expert in the subject you're talking about, you shouldn't delude your audience by saying you are; but you wouldn't have been asked to speak if your ideas or information weren't of interest. The fact that you're not marketing director of your company doesn't mean your knowledge of how to market your company's product is any less valid. If your photographs have never been published in a national magazine, that doesn't affect your ability to discuss photographic techniques.

I once listened to three executives from the head office of a giant corporation rehearsing presentations about their company which they were going to deliver to some computer experts. None of the executives was an expert in computers, but they were all powerful, influential men with no conceivable reason to apologize to anyone for their lack of expertise in one particular area. Yet each stood up and read his speech exerting no energy, no authority and no awareness. When they had finished, I said, "How do you expect a group of the nation's leading computer experts to believe that you're the top-level executives of a powerful corporation when you can barely be heard and are unable even to look an audience in the eye?

"You don't show your respect for your audience's credentials by suppressing your own. You show respect by preparing your speech thoroughly, delivering it with energy, and demonstrating you're willing to listen to them and their ideas."

Letting Yourself Come Through

All this relates back to the *S* of E.A.S.Y. Strength, or self-esteem, means having a strong, secure self-image. It means projecting the same you no matter who your audience is. I once conducted a seminar for a group of homemakers involved in volunteer work. When I said I projected the same me whether I was speaking to business executives, high school students or homemakers like themselves, one of the women argued that different people demand different responses: Her husband demanded a different her than her child did; her club work demanded a different her again, and so on. "I have to give them all what they want, don't I?" she concluded. As she said it, I looked at her and smiled and she heard what she was saying.

Sure, people are demanding and selfish and will try to take from us what they want and think they need. But each of us is only one person, and if we are secure within that person, we will present ourselves as we are to everyone we meet and let the chips fall where they may. It takes strength to always be honest about who and what we are, because it isn't always popular: Some people may not be able to accept our honesty, and decide they don't want to deal with us. But if we are direct and honest, we will know that the people who *do* deal with us really accept *us*, not some façade.

"But," you may be thinking, "surely we reveal different facets of our personality to different people, depending on the type of relationship we have. My boss, spouse, child, friend and business associates all see different sides of me." It's true that a business situation usually demands more control than a personal situation. It usually is not appropriate to act loving with a business associate, nor businesslike with a friend. But if you really want to learn to communicate more effectively with other people, you have to take the risk of being more open in every situation—of letting more of yourself come through. If your self-image is strong and secure, you will not be afraid to project the same *essential* you to every person you communicate with.

A businessman was incredulous when I said I used the same style of delivery with a group of high school kids as I did with top-level executives. "Do you mean to tell me," he said, "that if you were addressing a group of MBA's from Harvard, you would speak to them in exactly the same way you would to a group of tenth-graders?" I replied that the subject matter, or at least my approach to it, would differ, but my style of delivery would be the same; I wouldn't change the way I dress, and I wouldn't try to project a different image.

On a Par with Others

A mature, positive self-image means you consider yourself equal to other people, no matter what their socioeconomic status, position or personal accomplishments. If you feel you are on a par with other people, you will not subordinate yourself to one person, act condescending to the next, apologetic to another, and so on. Take your boss, for example. Your job is subordinate to his, but you shouldn't have to subordinate yourself as a person to him. If you're responsible and capable in your job, you can be direct with him and ask to be treated as an equal without being insubordinate, intimidating or aggressive. Many people play a subservient role with their boss because they think he demands it. I believe most employers will accept directness from an employee if it comes with respect and sensitivity. The same principle applies in your relationship with your spouse, child, friend or business associate—and when you are speaking to a group.

A positive self-image does not mean being an egotist. The egotistical person does not consider himself equal to others; he considers himself superior and will not respect the integrity of the other person's self-image. When a speaker disagrees with his audience he should be able to criticize the other person's point of view without attacking him as a person. I learned this lesson painfully when I did a television interview with the editor of a newspaper at Kent State University in the late sixties, during the days of the student unrest. I was emotionally involved with the issue and considered the man's editorials about the student dissidents biased and inaccurate. I went into the interview silently exulting about how I was going to destroy this unethical bigot. I was sarcastic, condescending and hostile throughout the interview. I made a fool of the man and made him squirm before the viewers.

When it was over, I was shaking. One of the producers at the station came up to me and said, "Sandy, you didn't have to attack him like that. All you had to do was ask him direct questions and let him destroy himself. You didn't have to pound the guy into the ground.

"I don't agree with the way he has been covering the riots either, but I found myself sympathizing with him during the interview because you were so nasty."

Instead of criticizing his actions, I had gone for his jugular and tried to knock down his self-image. Doing so was self-defeating because it reflected my lack of sensitivity to another human being instead of the editor's lack of sensitivity to the disaffected students.

We All Need "Strokes"

But no matter how "together" we are—confident in our abilities but not unrealistic about them, aware of our weaknesses but not immobilized by that self-knowledge—we should never forget that everyone's self-image is fragile. There is a limit to the amount of criticism any of us can take before our self-confidence falters.

If you understand that everyone needs positive reinforcement, or "strokes," as transactional analysis calls it, you will recognize the times you need strokes and actively seek them when you do. If your image of yourself as a speaker is shaky or if you have a couple of unpleasant speaking experiences, go out of your way to speak to a group you know will be receptive.

A businessperson who is increasingly called upon to speak could volunteer to conduct a seminar sponsored by the Small Business Administration for persons starting their own businesses. This audience would be receptive because they would be eager to pick up tips from the established businessperson. A reporter unaccustomed to speaking could give a talk on careers in journalism to a group of high school students interested in the field. People tend to be intimidated when they have to speak to a group of their peers, because they feel the audience knows as much or more about their subject than they do; so an attorney elected president of his bar association could bolster his self-confidence by speaking to service organizations such as the Kiwanis Club or the Rotary Club. If a new president of a parent-teacher association is nervous about speaking to a group of adults, he could begin by speaking to the students in the school. An executive nervous about getting up on his feet in front of a group could teach a Sunday school class, a Boy Scout troop, or a youth group at the local Y.M.C.A.

Small successes are excellent proving grounds for larger ones in the future.

A Test of Your Perceptions

Answering the following questions about yourself should help you gain a better understanding of the interaction that takes place between you and your audience.

1. Take an honest look at who you are. Write down a description of yourself under each of these three headings:

Your Public Self	*Your Private Self*	*Your Ideal Self*
(the person you think your audience sees)	(your self-image: who you think you are)	(who you wish you were)

Examine the discrepancies above. How might these discrepancies affect you in certain speaking situations? As you read this book, ask yourself what you can do about them.

2. Make a list of your strengths and weaknesses as they relate to effective speaking. Ask a close friend or business associate to do the same. If the lists are significantly different, ask yourself why this person sees you differently: Are you doing things that leave people with an image of you that is different from the way you feel inside? (For example: You think you're a warm person. A coworker says you intimidate him. Why?)

3. Do you have pet peeves about people (men, women) in general? What are they? What do your complaints tell you about you?

4. Do people have pet peeves about you? What are they? What do you think you can do about them?

5. List ideas you have received in the past from parents, teachers, friends, about how you *should* speak, how you should stand, about exerting energy in a speaking situation, about reaching out to people, about how you look or move.

How do these ideas affect you as you approach a speaking situation today? If they affect you negatively, can you make specific plans to change your ideas about how you should speak?

6. Think about a speaker you admire. Why do you think he's effective? Could you develop any of the characteristics he possesses? How?

5

What Are You Afraid Of?

How to Relax

Almost everyone who has ever stood up to speak in front of a group knows what stage fright means. The demon stage fright can assume many forms. It can mean queasy stomach, weak knees, dry mouth, shaky legs, light head, sweaty hands or an overwhelming "out-of-it" feeling with unpredictable, sometimes disastrous, results—such as walking away from a microphone instead of toward it, walking into a wall or, dread of all dreads, "going blank."

If fear of stage fright has made you turn down opportunities to express yourself in front of a group, think for a moment about the speeches you have heard. How often have you seen a speaker so nervous he couldn't catch his breath? How often have you seen a speaker whose mind went blank for a really long time? Have you ever seen a speaker faint or throw up? Have you ever seen an audience boo a speaker off the stage?

You've probably never seen any of these awful things happen, except perhaps the latter, if you've attended a volatile political rally with a really hostile audience.

So what are you afraid of?

You're afraid you won't be perfect. You are your own worst critic and you're afraid you won't be as good as you think you should be. You get up in front of an audience and look out and see one person frowning and immediately you assume everyone is against you or thinks your ideas childish or stupid. Or you stumble over a couple of words and immediately you think, "Well, now I've blown it. I might as well give up."

The Importance of Being Imperfect

For me, the intellect is always the guide but not the goal of the performance. Three things have to be coordinated and not one must stick out. Not too much intellect because it can become scholastic. Not too much heart because it can become schmaltz. Not too much technique because you become a mechanic. Always there should be a little mistake here and there—I am for it. The people who don't do mistakes are cold like ice. It takes risk to make a mistake. If you don't take risk, you are boring.

—Vladimir Horowitz*

You engage in dozens of conversations every day, many of them just as important—or more so—than the occasional speech you deliver. Yet you never think for a moment that your conversation should be polished or perfect, delivered without any hesitations, pauses, repetitions, rephrasings or silences.

* From Helen Epstein's "The Grand Eccentric of the Concert Hall," *The New York Times Magazine*, January 8, 1978.

If you approach a speech thinking that, contrary to the normal dynamics of conversation, it has to be polished and perfect, of course you'll be consumed with stage fright. Common sense will tell you your goal is impossible to attain, so panic is a perfectly natural reaction. The first step toward controlling stage fright is remembering that getting a message across to an audience means being involved with your subject and caring about your audience. You don't have the remotest chance of accomplishing this if you regard a speech as a formal succession of words to be delivered precisely and flawlessly. If you do, you ignore three things: that you are in a dynamic situation, that you are a human being, and that you are talking to people.

Your aim is not perfection. That doesn't mean you should not prepare your speech carefully. Thorough preparation is the second step toward relaxation. You'll be a lot more relaxed in a speaking situation if you've thought through and carefully planned what you're going to say. I will discuss preparation in detail in Chapter 9, but one aspect can be of special help in overcoming tension. Having a well-rehearsed beginning and ending to your speech is important to overcoming stage fright as you begin to speak, and to maintaining the confidence that you will make it through to the end. A strong beginning that "hooks" your audience and makes them sit up and listen will help you relax because you will immediately establish control over the situation. Knowing that you are going to end your talk with equal punch will help you maintain momentum throughout the body of your speech. Also, if something unexpected occurs and you must wrap up quickly, you will know immediately what to say.

Next, remember, you would not have been invited to speak if you were not recognized as some kind of authority on your subject. If the audience felt they had nothing to learn from you, they wouldn't be there. Even if you speak to a group that you know disagrees with your views, the audience still is interested in hearing you or they wouldn't be there. Stage fright is such a universal experience that audiences actually empathize with the way it feels to be standing alone, the focus of an entire group's attention. So stop considering the audience the adversary, ready to pounce on your every slip.

Because communication is two-way, the audience absorbs and reflects your state of mind. If you're nervous, they will be nervous, too. They want you to be comfortable so that they can be comfortable. Remember that the audience is just people, essentially on your side—even if they don't agree with everything you have to say.

Finally, remember that while practice will not make perfect—nor should it—we learn by doing. Speaking in public will get easier the more often you do it.

Physical Relaxation

Relaxation begins mentally, by developing a more objective understanding of what the speaking situation involves and by setting realistic goals.

But we are not completely rational creatures. Our minds are rarely in full control of our emotions or our bodies. Because mind, emotion and body are so closely related and interdependent, I approach relaxation first from a physical standpoint: Gaining control of the body is the first step toward gaining control of mind and feeling.

People often say, "You've got to be tense if you want to achieve," pointing to the "keyed-up" feeling that accompanies a major effort or challenge. The feeling of mental and physical alertness we get in moments of stress, such as just before delivering a speech, is an automatic physiological reaction to stress, caused by adrenaline being pumped into our bloodstream.

Digestion stops, our heart speeds up, we breathe harder, we perspire, and our mouth dries out.

It's true that that surge of adrenaline sharpens our physical and mental capabilities and inspires us to perform at our best, but I don't consider this tension. I prefer to look at it as a surge of energy, which if properly channeled releases the tension within the speaker so that it can work for him instead of against him.

WHAT TENSION IS

Tension is blocked energy. It is what happens when a speaker holds his energy in instead of letting it out. Visualize tension as a clenched fist. It results from holding—physically, mentally or emotionally. This chapter should show you how to relax that fist and release the tension.

I do not believe that you are going to be tense no matter what when you speak to a group. Speech teachers who believe tension is inescapable sometimes prescribe gimmicks to concentrate tension in an unobtrusive place—such as tensing up your toes so that your hands will be free, or pressing your thumb up against your index finger so that your face can be happy. I believe that gimmicks like these are unnecessary because we *can* rid our bodies of tension.

We physically release tension when we exhale. A physiological explanation of how this works is included in the next chapter. Because breathing out allows a physical release of tension, learning how to breathe while under stress is an effective way to decrease tension.

Negative anticipation makes you experience tension at the beginning of a speech. Instead of focusing on what is happening here and now and dealing with it, you think of what might happen five minutes from now, when you have been introduced and are about to begin speaking, or twenty minutes from now, when you have finished speaking and someone asks a question. Five minutes later, when you are approaching the microphone, you're not thinking about the business at hand, which is getting settled in a balanced position and looking out at your audience. You are thinking, What if the audience doesn't like me? What if they notice the pimple on my nose? What if I can't remember what to say? What if nobody listens?

Focusing on your own breathing is the most effective method I know for focusing on the here and now. Breathing is an essential, central rhythm of your body, so focusing on your breathing means getting back in touch with yourself.

The following breathing exercise lowers adrenaline levels, slows your heartbeat, and releases physical tension. It also releases mental and emotional tension by focusing the mind first on the here and now, and then on a successful outcome of a speech. It will take ten to fifteen minutes as described below.

AN EXERCISE FOR ENERGETIC RELAXATION

The goal of this exercise is "energetic relaxation." Its aim is not to "let it all hang out," slouch, daydream, sleep, hypnotize yourself or become passive; it is to concentrate without tension on the here and now.*

1. Sitting in a straight-backed chair, go through some simple movements to relieve tension in your body: Stretch fully; move your arms over your head; bend your spine; roll your head gently in circles.

2. Consciously choose to let go. Make this an active decision. Talk yourself into it; tell yourself that this is the most important thing you can possibly do for the next few minutes.

* You may want to put these directions on a cassette tape, leaving time between them to do the exercise.

3. Center your body parts. Start with your head and work down through the major body parts—neck, chest, stomach, hips, legs, feet. To center each part, mentally locate the exact three-dimensional center and align it with the plumb line of your body. For example, to center your head, imagine it to be a ball balanced on a broomstick; move it until you mentally feel the point of balance. Do not stiffen. As you allow your body parts to line up vertically, feel how your body settles and relaxes. Let every part of your body feel heavy. This is what I call "settling in."

4. Exhale deeply. See how deeply and completely you can let your breath out. As the air nears what seems to be the end, try to let out just a little more air; if you can let a little more out, you will notice a tremendous reduction in tension. You are not trying to force or control your breath: This is a letting go, a releasing, a giving up. You should be able to feel your ribcage dropping with each exhale. Exhaling in this way should feel like a deep sigh. Do this several times.

5. Scan through your body to pick up points of tension, the way radar scans for disturbances. When you detect tension or discomfort, see if you can think it away. Tell your body to go limp around the point of tension and to release it from your body. Do this until you no longer find any points of tension.

6. Now that your body is relaxed, your mind focused, and both are working for you together, visualize yourself just after successfully delivering a speech. Think of the audience applauding you, of individuals you respect complimenting you, of feeling good about yourself. Really let yourself feel the afterglow of a successful speech.

Practice this routine twice a day for a couple of weeks or until you have mastered the steps and can go through them effortlessly, without consciously thinking about each one. When the sequence is second nature to you, you will be able to go through the basic steps (1–4) of centering, settling in, and exhaling in a few seconds. Do it in any moment of stress—in a traffic jam, an argument, just before an important meeting. Do it in the car on your way to give a speech. Do it when you're being introduced. When you stand up, take a moment to breathe, center and settle before you begin to speak. And during the speech, go through the sequence any time you feel the need to pause, relax and get back with yourself for a moment.

You may think this exercise seems too simplistic to be effective. But believe me, it does work. It has helped hundreds of my students overcome tension when they speak. Sometimes the results have been dramatic. One student found it such an effective way to relax that, as an added benefit, he was able to give up smoking. When Chip, a real estate salesman, spoke the first time, he was almost literally in the air. He had such an excess of nervous energy his whole body was "up," from his springy steps to his raised shoulders. He spoke so fast he slurred his words. He used plenty of gestures, but they were so overdone that they were distracting and detracted from what he said. One evening, while in the middle of one of his excessively animated talks, he turned, walked away from the lectern, paused, and exhaled so loudly the whole class noticed the sound and the videotape picked it up. When he walked back, he was visibly "down"—infinitely more relaxed both in his body and voice.

This breathing exercise will help you achieve the kind of relaxation you need before giving a speech. It is not the kind of relaxation you feel when you're dancing, sprawled on a sofa in front of a television set, or about to fall asleep. I call it "energetic relaxation" because it means letting out your energy instead of holding it in as you do when you are under tension. Energetic relaxation is the feeling of openness and responsiveness that comes when nothing is blocking your ability to respond. Energetic relaxation is alert; it concentrates on the here and now. It is relaxation while under stress—without tension.

Body and Mind Together

Energetic relaxation can be achieved only when body and mind are working together. The close correlation of body and mind is never more obvious than when we speak. Our physical reactions to stage fright graphically illustrate how responsive our bodies are to our minds. And when our minds go blank during a talk, it's very often a mental reaction to physical tension.

The method of stress control called biofeedback training demonstrates the intertwining of body and mind, and the ability of the mind to control the body through increased awareness. A person undergoing biofeedback training is connected to one or more sensitive biofeedback devices that record his physical reactions to stress, as manifested in muscle tension, skin temperature and brain activity. Then he relives a stressful scenario—for example, an argument with his boss—at the same time watching how his body reacts. Once he becomes aware of exactly how different parts of his body react to stress, he puts his mind to work to control his physical reactions. Biofeedback experts claim outstanding success using this method.

There is nothing magic about biofeedback training. It is self-awareness that enables biofeedback patients to control stress, not a complicated machine. The machines simply make the person aware of how his body reacts to stress.

You can demonstrate the same point without a biofeedback machine by going through this exercise: Stand in a centered position with your arms stretched out level with your shoulders at right angles to your body. Without moving your feet, swing your arms first to the right and then to the left as far as you can comfortably go. Observe the point on the wall where your arms stop. Let your arms fall by your sides, close your eyes, and imagine your arms going through the same movement, but reaching farther. Repeat the movement. Did your arms move farther the second time? If so, it is because your mind worked on it.

Because body and mind are so closely related, you cannot have an efficient mind without an efficient body. People today are generally much more aware of the importance of physical fitness to mental and emotional health than they used to be. I'm sure you've read plenty on the subject. I will only add that physical exercise helps to release the physical tension that prevents you from speaking your best. A fit body makes it easier to relax when you speak. Exercise should be as integral a part of your daily routine as brushing your teeth and combing your hair. If you hate the sight of a gymnasium or track shoe, simply consider it your daily medicine. It's as important to your efficiency, alertness and effectiveness as a speaker as is getting enough sleep.

Getting in Touch with Your Body

But there is more than physical fitness to being in control of your body when you speak. To really learn how to relax and be in control of the speaking situation, you must be in touch with your body. Exercise tones your muscles, decreases your pulse rate, and makes your heart more efficient, but it doesn't necessarily tune you in to your body. It doesn't necessarily make you sensitive to points of tension in your body or how your body looks when you move it in certain ways—both of which are important to how much in control of your body and how relaxed you are when you speak.

When I started teaching, at the age of eighteen, I began to feel real tension for the first time in my life. I started getting massages, which helped relieve the tension and taught me to differentiate feelings in different parts of my body and to understand how individual parts felt when they were relaxed. Since then, I have been involved in calisthenics, modern dance, jogging and yoga, and a specialist in body movement has made me aware of how I tend to hold in tension through my shoulders and neck. I now am so completely tuned in to my body that I don't have to wait until I'm suffering from a stiff neck to know I've been holding in tension. I can feel the tension in my neck when it begins, and I can tell myself to exhale, to let go, and to release the tension before it spreads throughout my body.

Becoming attuned to your body is a very individual thing. I cannot give you a prescription for it, but I can make some general recommendations which you can tailor to your own needs and lifestyle. I encourage people who are very inhibited, who have never learned to express themselves physically, to get into an activity that helps them express their individuality, such as dancing, fencing, yoga, gymnastics or calisthenics that concentrate on body form rather than rapid movement.

Being in touch with your body opens up new areas of awareness. When you're in touch with your body, you will quickly become aware of points of tension and be able to deal with them. It will also help you gain more control of your body when you speak.

Centering and Settling

Good posture is essential to relaxation, but it is not the chest-out, shoulders-back, stomach-in kind of posture you probably have been taught. Good posture on your feet means centering and settling in, just as you did when sitting in a chair during the energetic relaxation exercise.

To center when standing, think of an imaginary axis running through your body. When you are centered, your feet are solidly planted, a few inches apart. Your feet are directly under your shoulders, inside your armpits, giving structural support. Head, shoulders and chest are directly over one another. Your chest is up, neither thrown out nor caved in. You can feel the floor firmly under you, through the balls and heels of your feet.

Hang a string down the center of a full-length mirror. Stand in front of it and see how your body could be perfectly bisected by the string if you were centered. Take the time to feel the difference between having your head cocked to one side, or having one shoulder lower than another, and being really centered and settled into the floor.

In classes, I ask each student to stand in front of the group and center and settle in and assume a balanced, relaxed posture. Men often say they feel as if they are slouching or, as one man put it, "like a bag of feed." A student who had been in the army said he felt as if he had lost his moral fiber when he wasn't standing with his shoulders pulled back. He felt relaxed, of course, and he *looked* perfectly erect.

Men have been taught all their lives to pull their shoulders back and throw their chest out; women have been taught to hold their stomachs in. Both postures are uncomfortable and interfere with relaxation when standing. Men and women should stand in exactly the same way, with their feet supporting their body directly under their shoulders. If you are a woman and think that this centered, relaxed stance might not look "ladylike" when you are wearing a skirt, test it in front of a mirror. I think you'll agree that it looks natural and comfortable and doesn't detract from your femininity.

Gestures and Body Movement

Natural movement when you speak also will help you relax. The important thing is to allow yourself to be natural, to let movements happen. Standing rigidly with your hands by your sides for twenty minutes is not natural, nor is swaying from one foot to the other or walking with tiny, mincing steps.

Because many of us are so uptight physically and so out of touch with our bodies, our bodies send out different messages than our mouths when we find ourselves in a new or uncomfortable situation, such as speaking to a group. When I ask students to describe something that makes them laugh, something that makes them happy, and something that makes them sad, their faces are often serious when they describe a humorous event and they often smile apologetically when they describe a tragedy in their lives.

To help students loosen up their bodies when they speak, I ask them to assume the persona of a soap-box orator or somebody comparable. Or I ask them to speak in a nonsense language and convey their meaning in gestures and tone of voice instead of words. After going through these exercises, students usually say they felt silly but they also felt much more relaxed. The physical movement relaxed their bodies, helping them to relax mentally and emotionally as well. And it helps them realize that the body wants to gesture—if you let it. When you're energized by the content of your message, your body will naturally want to express that energy. And your body expresses its energy through gestures and movement.

Many books on speech go into great detail about how and when to move and gesture. I say, "Let go, move, and let the gestures happen." Because I believe that movement and gestures should happen naturally, I don't specify ways to punctuate certain kinds of ideas or feelings. But in general, if you make a fuller gesture, take a larger step, or move more slowly, you will send out a more relaxed total body message.

Using your body to release energy is a learned activity. If you are not used to expressing yourself physically, you can learn to do it.

Energetic Silence

When you exhale, center and settle, what you are really doing is "getting with" yourself before you focus out on your audience. As I said in Chapter 3, effective speaking depends on a balance of speaker, message and audience. The nervous speaker tends to focus on himself or his message at the expense of his audience. Overcoming tension means coming to terms with yourself first, in order to overcome the self-consciousness that results from too much emphasis on the self. Only then can you effectively focus out on your audience.

But there must always be a balance: You never focus all your energy out. Periodically throughout the speech, you should pause, breathe, and get back with yourself.

Don't be afraid of the silent moment that occurs when you do this. If you can control silence you will control the speaking situation. In my seminars, I put students through an exercise in which they stand behind the lectern, exhale, settle, center, then walk away from the lectern with assertive strides, stop, center, settle, and pause. During this whole sequence, they have not said a word and the audience's attention has been focused on them. After an "energetic silence," during which the student establishes eye contact with each member of the audience, he makes a statement. Then he turns around, walks halfway back toward the lectern, turns around again to face the audience, centers, settles in, pauses, and makes another statement before turning once again and returning to the lectern.

This exercise teaches students that walking on silence is an act of assertion. The longer they can hold the silence, the more power they feel. The tense, insecure speaker dreads silence and will do anything he can to fill it up. He uses fillers such as "um," "you know," "okay," and "now." He rushes from one sentence to the next, instead of finishing each with a push and letting it stand on its own. If you're giving out energy, you don't need joiners for your ideas. If you're involved with what you're saying, the energy you speak with will allow each statement to stand alone.

Pause is one of the most effective ways a speaker can emphasize a point. Using pause for emphasis is what I call an energetic silence, because the speaker has been speaking energetically and forcefully and the silence makes the audience sit up and actively anticipate his next statement. You have a right to pause; you have a right to silence. Pause is also one of the most effective ways to relax in the middle of a speech, because it gives you time to breathe and get back with yourself. I'm often asked, "What do I do if my mind goes blank?" You can do several things: You can pause and check your notes; you can pause and establish eye contact with your audience while you compose your thoughts; you can pause and ask a question to divert attention away from yourself for a moment; or you can pause, walk back to the lectern (if you have moved away from it), exhale, center, settle in, check your notes, and if after all that you still haven't thought of any way to continue, you can say, "My mind has gone blank. Can someone help me by repeating what I just said?"

A middle-aged housewife attended a seminar when she was elected president of her parent-teacher association. She was extremely nervous about speaking on her feet, so much so that her voice shook and she couldn't catch her breath. After learning the breathing techniques for relaxation, she tried them out when her car stalled in busy downtown traffic. "I was holding up traffic and everyone was honking at me," she recalled. "Ordinarily I would have gone to pieces. Instead, I focused on the exhale, got with myself, and calmed down while I struggled to get the motor going. It really worked." Toward the end of the seminar, she had to speak to the PTA. "When I got up," she told the class, "people were talking. I forced myself to keep quiet instead of trying to yell above the crowd. They continued to talk and I kept focusing on the exhale. Before I knew it, they were all quiet and there they were—all two hundred of them—waiting for *me* to speak. It was such a feeling of power, I couldn't believe it."

A little silence is a powerful thing.

Dealing with the Reality

Because tension means holding in emotionally as well as physically, it interferes with open expression. Open expression means letting out your feelings as well as letting your body move freely. If someone is doing something that annoys you and you don't tell him about it, you feel tense because you are holding in your feelings. When you're speaking to a group, the same principle can make you tense. For example, if a waiter is serving dessert and the clatter of dishes is annoying you, you will become increasingly tense if you ignore it and try to speak above it. If, instead, you say, "My voice really can't compete with those noisy plates, so I'll wait until you've all been served your desserts before I continue," you have expressed your feelings and released your tension. Or if someone comes in late and interrupts you with questions that have already been answered, you can say, "I think that question was answered before you came in. If you don't mind, I'll move on and discuss it with you later."

I call this "dealing with the reality." To deal with the reality you must be firmly rooted in the here and now. The breathing exercise described earlier will help you to do this. Dealing with reality relates to my concept of strength, because being open with your audience in this way lets them know who and what you are.

Dealing with the reality also means being straight when you

goof. If you trip over the microphone cord, simply move it and go on; if you stumble over a word, say "That wasn't clear; I'll repeat it." Speakers dread bloopers but their reaction to them often is far more embarrassing than the blooper itself. Admitting an error, not being afraid to smile at it if it's funny, apologizing if it's appropriate, but not dwelling on it, is what I mean by being direct and dealing with the reality.

Self-Image and Relaxation

Once in a while I have a student who cannot overcome his nervousness even after practicing all these relaxation techniques over an extended period of time. Usually the reason is his self-image. It's normal to be nervous and self-conscious when you're not used to speaking to a group; but if you're prepared, and practice proper breathing, standing, movement, and all the other relaxation techniques I suggest, and you still freeze every time you're in the spotlight, it probably says more about your feelings about yourself than it does about the speaking situation. The more in tune you are with who you are—the more you respect and like who and what you are—the more comfortable you will be in any situation. Conversely, the more things you don't like about yourself, the harder it will be to get up in front of an audience and let yourself be the focus of attention.

After attending two seminars, a very bright woman still couldn't look an audience in the eye or bear being the object of people's attention. I finally suggested to her that she see a psychologist, because her problems were too deep-seated for me to deal with.

Sometimes the problem can be a person's visual self-image. An attractive but overweight woman told me in the middle of a seminar that she was afraid she wasn't going to benefit from it at all because whenever she saw herself on videotape she couldn't focus on energy level, body movement or anything else that related to how effectively she was speaking. All she could see was the fat. As it happened, she made up her mind to lose weight—and did. Losing weight was her personal prerequisite to becoming a more effective speaker. It didn't matter how many tried and tested relaxation techniques she used; none was going to work until she was able to feel more positively about her visual image.

Being in control of your visual image—feeling comfortable and knowing you look good—will bolster your self-confidence and help you relax. Wear clothes you are physically comfortable in so that you can stand, sit, and move freely. Avoid pants, jackets, belts or skirts that are too tight, heels that are too high, skirts that are too short. Wear an outfit that you feel you look good in; but as a rule of thumb, don't wear an outfit for the first time. You may feel self-conscious in it and it may surprise you in a way you aren't prepared for: Perhaps it will crease when you sit down or a zipper will open, or a jacket will be difficult to gesture in because it fits too tightly across the back. Having your wardrobe under control will give you one less item to be concerned with.

Relaxation in Brief

LAYING THE GROUNDWORK

1. Remember: The more in tune you are with who you are—the more you respect and like who and what you are—the more comfortable you will be in any situation.

2. To relax mentally, you must be physically relaxed. Develop a daily exercise regimen. And get in touch with your body through some activity that helps you express yourself

physically, so that you will understand how your body reacts to stress.

3. Practice the exercise for energetic relaxation until you can go through the steps automatically. Then *use* it during your everyday life in moments of tension.

PREPARING THE SPEECH

1. Practice not to make perfect but to gain full control of your ideas. Genuine confidence comes not from word-for-word memorization of a text, but from a thorough knowledge of your subject.

2. Carefully prepare a choreographed beginning and ending to your speech, and thoroughly rehearse them.

THE DAY OF THE SPEECH

1. Wear clothing you are comfortable in, and that you feel you look good in.

2. Go through the energetic relaxation exercise at home.

3. Practice the exhale in the car on the way to the speech.

4. Before you stand up to speak, remind yourself that the audience is just people. They want you to relax so that they can relax.

5. When you stand up to speak, take as much time as you need to center and settle into a balanced position, exhale, and get with yourself.

6. Throughout the speech, pause as often as you feel the need. Use silence, both to gain control over yourself and to give your audience time to absorb your ideas.

7. As you speak, deal with the reality. If someone or something is annoying you, deal with the situation directly. If you don't, tension will build inside you.

8. And remember: We learn by doing. Speaking will get easier the more often you do it.

Over the years, I have spent more and more time with students concentrating on relaxation and body movement. I cannot stress too much how important these are. Your body speaks forcefully. It is you. Understanding your body and learning how to make it work for you instead of against you is essential to becoming an effective speaker.

Important as they are, however, these relaxation techniques are not a cure-all or a guarantee that you will never again feel nervous or experience stage fright. You probably never will completely conquer stage fright. I still experience it at times, and it hits me when I least expect it. It's an irrational feeling that has nothing to do with the size of the audience or the importance of the occasion.

So practice the relaxation techniques in this chapter not to dispel nerves once and for all, but to enable you to cope with nervousness—or as physician Hans Selye puts it, to learn to experience stress without distress.*

* Hans Selye, M.D., *Stress Without Distress* (New York: J. B. Lippincott, 1974).

6

The Power of
Your Voice

As a student of speech and drama, in my teens, I studied the physiology of voice in great detail and spent countless hours doing formal exercises to develop my speaking voice. When I began teaching speech to people with completely untrained voices, I realized that a person who is energetic and involved with his subject and his audience doesn't necessarily need formal voice training to become an effective speaker. So I put less emphasis on voice training and exercises in my classes.

Now I have come full circle. I still believe you can be an effective speaker without doing a single voice exercise. But I also believe that voice should be given its due as one of the speaker's most important tools. As with his message, his posture, his body and his dress, he can choose whether or not to make the best of it. You can cut a tree down with a dull axe, but if you hone the cutting edge to its finest and sharpest, you will cut the tree down more neatly, more precisely, and with much greater control.

I have already said that your delivery is more important than the words you use. Your voice is the medium of your delivery; without it, there would be no speech. The Gettysburg Address would have been words to the wind if it was not heard. The quality of your voice can greatly enhance—or detract from—your audience's attentiveness.

Voice, as distinguished from speech, is a natural medium of emotional expression. Animals and infants cannot talk, but they use voice to express their feelings of hunger, fear, contentment and anger. Because the sound of a person's voice reflects his feelings about what he is saying, we interpret what a person really means by his words by listening to his voice.

Most people are totally unaware of their own voices. Yet your voice says so much about you to your world. It reflects who and what you are.

When we respond positively or negatively to a voice, what we really are doing is responding positively or negatively to the kind of person we think that voice represents. To an audience, the voice is the person. A soft, whispery voice reflects a gentle, childlike person; a dull monotonous voice reflects a phlegmatic, tedious person; a tight, high-pitched voice reflects a nervous, inhibited person; a harsh, strident voice reflects an abrasive, aggressive person; a full, melodious voice reflects an expressive, responsive person in harmony with himself and his world.

You can make your voice work for you. And knowing it is working for you can increase your self-confidence immeasurably.

But, you may be thinking, isn't the sound of your voice something innate, something you are born with? After all, men's voices are naturally lower than women's. We can change the sound to get our meaning across, but we can't change the basic tone or natural range, can we?

Yes and no. Yes, men's voices in general are naturally lower

than women's, because their vocal cords are longer and
thicker than women's. But each of us, man or woman, has a
wide natural range of pitch and tone. How we develop it depends on our environment and our "programming," as I defined it in Chapter 4. The woman who can barely be heard
when she asks a question at a meeting doesn't necessarily lack
physical vocal power to project her voice; she may lack the
self-confidence to do so. A whiny voice reflects querulousness;
a heavy voice reflects authoritativeness; a soft voice timidity.

The sound of our voice reflects how we have *chosen* to let
our world see us. Whether or not what we have chosen to let
people see is what really is going on inside us is a different
matter. Remember the "apologizer" described in Chapter 3—
the president of a multinational company, a physically large
man who was afraid he would intimidate people if he let the
authority of his position show in his voice? He was afraid to
expose his real self, and one way he tried to hide it was by the
sound of his voice. A reporter once told me he had imagined
me to be much older than I am when he talked to me on the
telephone, because my voice carried a lot of authority. I haven't
done any formal voice exercises for fifteen years. My voice is
stronger, more mature, and heavier than the voices of most women
my age because as I have grown and become more sure of myself
as a woman and as a person I have not been afraid to let people see
the strength I feel inside. I no longer feel the need to talk in the
stereotyped "female" voice.

Breathe to Free Your Voice

To understand how to make the best of your voice, you must
have a basic understanding of its physiology, which goes back
to breathing. When the lungs need air, the intercostal muscles

between the ribs contract and the ribs swing up and out. The diaphragm (an umbrella-shaped muscle just below the lungs which separates the chest from the abdomen) contracts, then descends and flattens, causing a slight displacement of the abdominal organs and an expansion of the upper part of the abdomen. The size of the chest cavity is increased and air rushes in to fill the vacuum. During exhalation the muscles relax and return to a resting position and air is forced out of the lungs.

The importance of this is twofold: First, when we inhale, the diaphragm and other muscles are in a state of contraction; when we exhale, they relax and return to resting position. So inhalation is tensing, tightening; exhalation is relaxation, letting go. Second, the diaphragm controls the rate of exhalation, but the actual push comes from the upper abdominal muscles, sometimes called the "belt muscles." So air is pushed not from the throat or the lungs but from the abdomen.

To become aware of this push, put your hands on your abdomen, inhale, and then exhale all air. Keep exhaling until you are forced to inhale again. Feel the push against your hands.

What does all this have to do with voice production? Everything. Voice is produced on exhalation. As we exhale, the push from the abdomen forces air out of the lungs through the voice box, or larynx, which is located in the throat. The vocal cords inside the larynx vibrate as the air passes through, producing sound in much the same way breath blown through the mouthpiece of a clarinet sets up vibrations in the reed and produces sound.

So voice is produced by a push from the gut—not the throat. And since voice is produced on exhalation and exhalation means a physical relaxation, or letting go, of the muscles involved, speaking, in a very real physical sense, means letting go.

The basis of good voice production is relaxation—letting it happen the way it was intended to happen. Tension interferes with this natural process. Because voice is a function of body, tension anywhere in the body can interfere with voice; but the most common tension points involve the muscles surrounding the speech center in the neck, jaw, shoulders, throat and upper back.

RELAXING THE SPEECH CENTER

1. Stand tall as if commanded to attention, weight evenly supported on both feet. Tense all the muscles in your legs, throw your shoulders back, and open your eyes wide.

2. Stand at ease. Let your head fall forward on your chest, slowly. Round your back over. Let gravity carry you down as you relax your shoulders, arms, hands, waist and hips. Let everything hang. Sway gently, then slowly come up, rolling up one vertebra at a time.

3. Settle in (as described in Chapter 5). Make sure your shoulders are down and relaxed.

4. Let your head fall gently to the left. Gently reach your ear toward your shoulder, then return to center. Repeat to the right side. Then let your head fall forward and slowly reach your chin to your chest. Return to center. Let your head fall back (but not too far—you should be able to see your eyes in a mirror).

5. Bring both shoulders up to your ears. Gently circle all the way back, around and down. Repeat slowly several times. Inhale as you bring your shoulders up; exhale as you bring them down. Circle your shoulders in the opposite direction.

6. Clasp your hands behind your back and turn them palms out. Stretch your arms up and down. Let your head fall forward. Gently round your back over and stretch your arms up and down again.

7. If you still feel tension at the back of your neck, repeat the neck rolls.

8. Let your jaw drop. Inhale deeply until a yawn is induced. This is a relaxer. Enjoy it.

Next, become aware of what relaxed breathing feels like by doing the following exercise:

BECOMING AWARE OF RELAXED BREATHING

1. Lie on your back with your knees flexed. Relax. Let your shoulders go and press your lower back into the floor. Place a book on your stomach; watch it rise and fall as you inhale and exhale. Leave the book there and watch what happens when you cough, pant, sigh. Notice how much of your breathing activity is centered much lower in your body than you probably thought. Remove the book; continue sighing deeply. Are you still aware of the breathing activity taking place in your abdomen? If not, replace the book and start again. Don't work hard at this; just relax and let it happen.

2. Stand up and go through the settling-in process (see Chapter 5). Press a book against your abdomen, exhaling as you do so. Now inhale and exhale as you were doing lying down. Make sure your shoulders stay relaxed. Note how the book is pushed forward when you inhale and goes back when you exhale.

3. Put your hands where the book was. As you breathe, feel the activity at the front and side. Keep your upper chest still.

4. As you go about your daily activities, become more aware of your breathing. Practice step number 3 for a few moments each day. Remember, you're really not learning anything new. You're simply learning to stop interfering and get back to the way you were meant to breathe.

Since voice is produced on exhalation, it follows that the more controlled and steady the exhalation, the more controlled and steady the voice. Exhalation for relaxation, as described in the last chapter, and exhalation for good voice production differ in one important way: Exhalation for relaxation is a quick exhalation that you let go all at once; exhalation for voice production is sustained and controlled. When you feel tense before a speech, or when you pause during a speech, you use the quick, letting-go exhale. When you are speaking, you use the sustained, controlled exhale.

So the next step toward good voice production is learning to control the exhalation. You can begin with the following exercise:

BECOMING AWARE OF THE RELATIONSHIP BETWEEN EXHALATION AND RELAXATION

1. Inhale, say "one," then relax. Do not try to control your breathing. Notice that when you relax you exhale automatically. However, passive exhalation is inadequate for an effective voice. You must control the rate of exhalation.

2. Place your hands on your abdomen, inhale, and gradually release the air with an "S" sound. Keep the sound and volume consistent. Notice the activity in your abdomen.

3. Place your hands on your abdomen once again, inhale, and release the air with an "S" sound. But this time, instead of keeping the volume consistent, place pressure on the exhaled breath. Notice how the volume increases as you put pressure on the exhaled air.

Some people, in spite of being relaxed and having a well-supported breath, still have weak voices that do not project. One cause of this is breathiness, or wasted breath, which can be an indication of a physical problem—for example, growths on the vocal cords. Because of this, a chronically breathy voice should be checked out by a physician.

Usually the cause is inefficient voice production, so that breath is wasted before vocalizing begins and also during production of various sounds. We hear this in vowels following the letter H—as in *hit, high, who*—and also S and SH and F, as, for example, in the words *sob, sister, assistance, should, for, fifty.*

As you practice any of these exercises check for wasted breath.

CONTROLLING THE EXHALE

You should never fade out at the end of a sentence because of insufficient breath. When you run out of breath, stop talking and breathe. Practice controlling your exhale with the following:

1. Inhale. Repeat a series of *ho* sounds until all your breath is exhaled. Notice the action of your abdominal muscles.

2. Read the following poem, breathing only at the ⋀ marks. Be sure your throat is relaxed.

Do you remember an Inn,
Miranda?
Do you remember an Inn? ⋀
And the tedding and the spreading
Of the straw for a bedding,
And the fleas that tease in the High Pyrenees,
And the wine that tasted of tar? ⋀
And the cheers and the jeers of the young muleteers
(Under the dark of the vine verandah)? ⋀
Do you remember an Inn, Miranda,
Do you remember an Inn? ⋀
And the cheers and the jeers of the young muleteers
Who hadn't got a penny,

And who weren't paying any,
And the hammer of the doors and the Din? ∧
And the Hip! Hop! Hap!
Of the clap
Of the hands ∧ to the twirl and the swirl
Of the girl gone chancing,
Glancing,
Dancing,
Backing and advancing, ∧
Snapping of the clapper to the spin
Out and in—
And Ting, Tong, Tang of the Guitar! ∧
Do you remember an Inn,
Miranda?
Do you remember an Inn?

—From "Tarantella," by Hilaire Belloc *

All voice improvement begins with breathing. Voice expresses our emotions, and breath is a barometer of our emotions. Consider for a moment how closely breath reflects our emotions: A slow, soft sigh means contentment; a heavy, full exhale, relief; a quick inhale, shock or fear; holding the breath, tension or anxiety. Laughing and crying are closely connected with breath: Actors learn to manipulate breath so that they can technically laugh or cry when they need to; women learn to control the pain of childbirth by controlling their breathing. Gaining control over your breathing really means gaining another measure of control over yourself.

* From *Sonnets and Verse by Hilaire Belloc* (New York: Robert M. McBride & Co., 1900).

The Five Main Aspects of Voice

Articulation

Breathing is the support mechanism for the sounds that come out of our mouths. The way we shape those sounds into meaningful words is called articulation. Each sound we form involves work by a different combination of the various organs of articulation, which include the lips, teeth, tongue, jaw and hard and soft palates. To sharpen your awareness of these organs, say the following consonants and diphthongs: *m, n, p, b, d, t, f, v, k, s, th* and *sh.* Note each time which organs form the sound.

Distinct articulation is important to voice not only so that we will be clearly and easily understood but also because it reflects our attitude toward what we are saying. Slurred, sloppy articulation often reflects jumbled thoughts, vague ideas or indifference toward our subject or audience, and often accompanies other lazy habits such as sloppy posture.

Articulation is closely related to energy. Few highly motivated people who really want to sell their message have poor articulation. One way the nervous or apathetic speaker transmits his insecurity or indifference is through poor articulation. Sloppy articulation frequently disappears once a speaker finds an appropriate energy level.

But careless articulation can also be nothing more than a bad habit. Some common Americanisms:

Dropping the *g* in *ing.* For example:

    runnin (running)
    havin (having)

Dropping *t* or *d* in the middle of a word. For example:

stard (started)
tweny (twenty)

Dropping *t* or *d* before or after *n*. For example:

they dono (they don't know)
I coun fine it (I couldn't find it)

BECOMING MORE AWARE OF DIFFERENT SOUNDS

Read the following words carefully:

b–p	ban pan	rabid rapid	nab nap
	bite pipe	hobbling hopping	cub cup
	bass pass		
t–d	toe dough	metal medal	fright fried
	tear dare	shutter shudder	sent send
	tug dug	fattest faddist	great grade
f–v	fast vast	rifle rival	half halve
	fan van	wafer waiver	safe save
	fat vat	baffle gavel	thief thieve
d–th	den then		
	dough throw		
	udder other		
s–z	sip zip	race raise	
	sue zoo	bus buzz	
v–w	vine wine		
	vest west		
	vile wile		
s–sh–ch	sum shum chum		
	seat sheet cheat		
	sue shoe chew		
r–w	rise wise		
	rain wane		
	rare ware		

g–ng	rag rang
	hag hang
	hug hung

The exercises below will make you more aware of how hard the articulators must work to produce distinct sounds. And because voice is a function of body, your body must work for you, too. Centering and settling, as described in the last chapter, are just as important to good voice production as they are to relaxation, because if your posture is not aligned, adequate abdominal breath support for distinct, clear articulation is impossible. It is difficult to articulate clearly if your posture is sloppy. Chip, the student described in the last chapter, whose nervousness gave him an excess of energy and resulted in an "up" posture, spoke so fast his words ran into one another. I recall another student, a hospital administrator who was very bright and had no trouble organizing and expressing his ideas, but whose posture prevented him from articulating clearly. He spoke with his chin thrust forward, his shoulders up and his chest caved in—a posture that made him look like a little old man. Try speaking while standing in that position and see how difficult it is to articulate clearly.

IMPROVING YOUR ARTICULATION

As you do the following exercises, make sure you have sufficient breath support and feel no strain in the throat. Be aware of the movement and position of the articulators; exaggerate the movement.

Say rapidly but clearly; repeating several times:

1. lee, lee, lee
2. la, la, la
3. tee, tee tee

4. ta, ta, ta
5. tee-lee, tee-lee, tee-lee
6. mee, mee, mee
7. ma, me, mi, mo, mu (long vowels)
8. We went away for a while.
9. gobble, gobble, gobble (Repeat rapidly. Open mouth wide on *ah* sound.)

Notice how much energy it takes to articulate clearly.

10. Read the following aloud, noting the consonant sounds:

Rats!
They fought the dogs and killed the cats
And bit the babies in the cradles,
And ate the cheeses out of the vats,
And licked the soup from the cooks' own ladles,
Split open the kegs of salted sprats,
Made nests inside men's Sunday hats,
And even spoiled the women's chats
By drowning their speaking
With shrieking and squeaking
In fifty different sharps and flats.

At last the people in a body
To the Town Hall came flocking:
"'Tis clear," cried they, "our Mayor's a noddy
And as for our Corporation—shocking
To think we buy gowns lined with ermine
For dolts that can't or won't determine
What's best to rid us of our vermin!
You hope, because you're old and obese,
To find in the furry civic robe ease?
Rouse up, sirs! Give your brains a racking

To find the remedy we're lacking,
Or, sure as fate, we'll send you packing!"
At this the Mayor and Corporation
Quaked with a mighty consternation.

An hour they sat in council;
    At length the Mayor broke silence:
"For a guilder I'd my ermine gown sell,
    I wish I were a mile hence!
It's easy to bid one rack one's brain—
I'm sure my poor head aches again,
I've scratched it so, and all in vain.
Oh for a trap, a trap, a trap!"
Just as he said this, what should hap
At the chamber-door but a gentle tap?
"Bless us," cried the Mayor, "what's that?"
—From *The Pied Piper of Hamelin,* by Robert Browning

Pitch

As I've said, the pitch of your voice—its highness or lowness—is not innate; every person has a wide natural range. The size of your vocal cords does determine the upper and lower limits of your range of pitch, however. Men's vocal cords are longer and thicker than women's, and so men's natural pitch is lower. But within this natural range, the pitch many people use is not their optimum pitch, but is often the pitch determined by habit, imitation (how often have you noticed members of the same family with similar pitches to their voices?), or even by tension in the jaw.

I often have accomplished, self-assured women in my classes who speak in sweet, little-girl voices. When they hear their voices on tape they usually realize that their voices do not reflect the authority and self-confidence they feel inside. Recognizing this discrepancy is the most important prerequisite to lowering the pitch of their voices to a level that more accurately reflects their inner selves. Of course, they also must understand how to breathe from the abdomen instead of pushing from the throat; find a more appropriate energy level; and apply my concept of strength to themselves in the speaking situation. But self-awareness is the most important part of this process.

Few people feel their voices are too low; almost always, the problem is too high a pitch. Generally, the faster you speak, the higher the pitch of your voice. So if you think your pitch is too high, try speaking more slowly. You may find your pitch lowers.

A high pitch can also be caused by tension in the vocal cords. As I have already emphasized, relaxation is the first step toward good voice production.

If you are dissatisfied with the pitch of your voice, try this exercise:

LOWERING YOUR PITCH

Tape record steps 1 and 5 and listen to the contrast.

    1. Say this sentence: "The quick brown fox jumps over the lazy dog."

    2. Let your jaw drop—relaxed, not stretched.

    3. Now "speak" the sentence with jaw dropped and tongue tip resting behind your lower teeth. You are finding full vocal tone without any articulation.

    4. Now "babble" the vowel sounds by freely moving your jaw up and down on each vowel of the sentence.

    5. Finally, return to the spoken word and say the sentence. Your jaw will be released and your voice will be relaxed and full. If tension has been raising your pitch, you will hear a deeper tone.

If you have a serious problem with pitch, consult a speech pathologist or laryngologist.

Inflection

Inflection is the way we vary the tone and pitch of our voice, according to our meaning. There are two basic types of inflection—upward and downward. A third—circumflex—is a combination of the other two. Since it is usually used with sarcasm (i.e., "Oh you did, did you?"), and since sarcasm has no place in effective communication, I choose to ignore it. A sentence, phrase or word with upward inflection either asks a question, requests information, asks for approval, or suggests uncertainty, insecurity, doubt, hesitancy or surprise. Downward inflection implies a mental attitude of certainty, strength, authority, command, defiance or assertion, and is used when information is being given rather than requested.

There is very little place for upward inflection in speaking to a group, because the speaker is not there to ask for reassurance from the audience; he is there to project authority. This must be balanced with audience awareness, of course, but the speaker, not the audience, should always control the speaking situation. (More about this in Chapter 8.)

Inflection can determine the meaning of what we say. The same words, depending on the inflection, can mean entirely different things. For example, "no" said with a long, downward inflection means something quite different from "no" with a questioning sound.

The most common kind of inappropriate upward inflection might more accurately be termed "middle inflection." When a person uses middle inflection his sentences never seem to end, nothing is punctuated, his voice sounds very indefinite, and everything blends together. He implies that something else is going to follow everything he says, *viz:* "We will focus on production, packaging and marketing." This statement would be much stronger if it were stated: "We will focus on production, packaging and marketing."

Even direct questions often can be asked more forcefully by dropping the tone of the voice at the end of the sentence. For example: "When are you going to do it?"

Often people inject too much upward inflection into their speech because a speech teacher once told them that they should vary their tone of voice to avoid a monotone or put more "personality" into their voice. I believe that being involved in and committed to what you are saying gives life to your voice—not superimposing a phony inflection. And speaking with downward inflection does not mean speaking in a monotone, because words with more than one syllable have their own inflection, from the stress on one syllable. For example:

Another reason speakers use too much upward inflection is that they are unsure of themselves and their message and are afraid to sound assertive and definite. Overrationalizing, unnecessary explanations, elaborations, *however*'s and *but*'s go hand in hand with upward inflection. "Nice guys" who have a problem establishing authority often use a lot of upward inflection. A marketing manager described by others in the seminar as just that, a nice guy, habitually ended his statements in a questioning tone and constantly bored the class with elaborate and unnecessary details. When he heard one of his long tedious tangents on videotape, he suddenly, for the first time, heard himself as others heard him. He remarked in astonishment, "Now I know why nobody has ever listened to me!"

I am not going to give any exercises for inflection because, of all the aspects of voice mentioned in this chapter, inflection is the most organic: It mirrors what is going on inside a person. It reflects a person's strength and self-esteem—whether he has the inner fiber to let the audience know he believes what he is saying, has no apologies, and will stand behind it.

The best way to check your inflection is to use a tape recorder. Over a period of time, tape yourself on the telephone, and tape yourself when practicing a speech. Then listen, asking yourself: Did that sound definite? Can I tell when a thought is completed? Does each sentence end with punch? Do I sound as if I believe what I am saying? Do I sound sure of what I am saying, or am I asking the audience to tell me it's OK?

Resonance

Another important aspect of voice is resonance. *Resono* in Latin means "I sound again." Resonance is the "resounding" of the sound created in the larynx in the chambers of the nose and throat. Resonance adds richness to the voice. Singers and actors spend a great deal of time developing it. The exercises that follow will not give your voice the resonance of a professional performer. However, they will help you develop a basic awareness of resonance and the two major problems related to it: nasality and denasality.

The main sources of vocal resonance are the throat, mouth, nasal cavities and chest. Again, tension works against the voice. Resonators must be open and relaxed to produce a pleasant, rich sound. For a full, pleasant voice, you must have a relaxed throat, relaxed jaw, flexible lips, flexible tongue and control of your soft palate.

IMPROVING YOUR RESONANCE

1. Achieve "settled-in" posture; inhale, and say the vowel sound *ah*.
2. Being sure your throat is relaxed, inhale, and hum the

consonant sound *mm*. Slowly open your mouth, trying not to change the tone, and let your jaw open wide until the sound becomes *ah*. Carefully close your mouth without stopping the sound as it again becomes *mm*. Continue to alternate *mm* and *ah* until your breath is gone. Note how much richer the *ah* sounds now than it did at first (1).

3. Inhale. Begin with *mm*, change to *ah*, and hold the sound steady as your diaphragm gradually relaxes. Notice the full rich sound. Be aware of all your resonating chambers.

4. Go through the same sequence with *mm* and each of the vowels, *a, e, i, o, u*. Repeat *mm* sound.

5. Because each of the following words begins with a nasal sound, there is a tendency to nasalize the vowels. Inhale, then project each word on one breath. Give the initial consonant full nasal resonance but do not nasalize the vowels.

my	nail	moose
might	nape	mail
night	neat	nap

6. Similarly, in words ending with a nasal sound there is a tendency to anticipate and nasalize the vowel immediately preceding it. Repeat the exercise with the following:

ran	town
ram	steam
room	calm
doom	dawn

NASALITY

You need some nasal resonance. An appropriate amount adds a musical quality to the voice; too much results in the unpleasant sound known as nasality.

Nasality plagues the speech of many Americans because of the way we draw out our vowel sounds, particularly the short *a* sound as in *bath* or *ran*. Nasality varies in intensity and degree from region to region and I generally don't believe people should change regional accents unless they are sloppy or offensive to the ear. But excessive nasality *is* offensive: Its twangy sound is harsh and unpleasant.

There are only three sounds that should be pushed through the nose instead of the mouth: *m, n,* and *ng*. To find out whether nasality has infected more sounds in your speech than these three, pinch your nose with two fingers and feel how your nose vibrates on the *m*'s, *n*'s and *ng*'s when you say *man, magazine, ran, rang* and *angry*. Pinch your nose again and say *bat, broth, task, seat, sigh, after, eye* and *row*. If you feel any vibrations this time, you have some unwanted nasality.

Nasality can be caused by tension in the throat and jaw. Accents that draw out vowel sounds (such as a Southern accent) also can cause nasality. Or it can be psychological: People who lack energy or mental commitment may suffer from lazy nasality, in which the soft palate hangs low so that too much sound escapes through the nose. People who feel they have no control over their lives often become whiners, and there are few sounds more nasal than a whine.

Nasality can be corrected with relaxed, proper breathing, adequate physical energy, and control of the soft palate. So the first step toward correcting nasality is going through the relaxation exercises outlined earlier in this chapter. Next, do the following exercises:

BECOMING AWARE OF NASALITY

1. Turn on your tape recorder. Say each word below four times. Open your mouth wide the first time; this makes it

hard for the soft palate to stay lowered and discourages nasality on vowel sounds. The fourth time, open your mouth as little as possible and deliberately nasalize the vowel.

time	dine
ham	him
man	mine
men	send

2. Repeat the words, nasalizing the vowels at random. Use the tape recorder to identify the nasal sounds.

CORRECTING NASALITY

Relax!

1. Read the words again, opening your mouth wider than usual on the vowel sounds. Check the recording for nasality.

STRENGTHENING THE SOFT PALATE

1. Repeat the following sounds several times. Notice how the soft palate lowers on *ng*.

Ng—ah, ng—ah, ng—ah

2. Vary with

Ng—oh, ng—oh, ng—oh
Ng—aye, ng—aye, ng—aye
Ng—eh, ng—eh, ng—eh

Avoid nasality on the vowels. Open your mouth wide.

3. Repeat the exercises, mouthing the sounds without making any sound. Feel the downward pull of the soft palate on *ng*.

4. Think of a wide-open throat, vocalizing a yawn, swallowing a tennis ball of air.

5. Record your voice reading different poems. Check for nasality.

DENASALITY

Nasality results from too much air being pushed through the nose. Denasality results from not enough air going through the nose. Many people confuse nasality and denasality. They say "I sound nasal because I have a cold," when in fact they sound denasal because the nasal passages are blocked. The vibrating air cannot resonate in the nasal chambers, so there is no nasal resonance.

Chronic denasality (as distinguished from the denasality a person suffers when he has a cold) almost always is a result of an organic problem—allergies, sinus problems, growths or a deviated septum (when the cartilage separating the nasal passages is crooked, blocking one passage). So if you suffer from denasality, you probably need help from a specialist of some kind. Try a throat specialist, an allergist or a speech pathologist.

Projection

People often come to me for help because they have trouble projecting their voice to a large group without becoming hoarse or getting a sore throat. A team of four men who were giving high-powered, concentrated, one-day seminars on time management all over the country came to me when they began to suffer from severe voice strain, to the point of actually losing their voices at times. They thought I could prescribe some magic voice exercises that would show them how to project without strain and allow them to maintain their hectic pace.

The first thing I did was question them about their daily schedule. It went like this: After an intensive, eight-hour seminar in one city, they would fly to the next, eat a big dinner, have a few drinks, and go to bed. A couple of them were heavy smokers; none of them exercised in any way at all. They expected to maintain a hectic, demanding schedule that heavily taxed their mental and emotional energies without any compensating outlet for the inevitable buildup of physical, mental and emotional tension.

When I have to maintain a schedule like that for a couple of weeks at a stretch, I make up my mind at the beginning that I will return home almost as fresh as when I leave. Each time I fly to a new city, I go directly to my hotel, unpack my sweat suit, and go outside and jog. If it's late and I'm unfamiliar with the city, I swim laps in the hotel pool.

There are plenty of ways to exercise while traveling without disrupting your schedule or even leaving your hotel. You can run flights of stairs, or jump rope or do calisthenics in the privacy of your room. My point is this: Because voice is a function of body, you cannot possibly expect to have a relaxed voice unless your body is relaxed. And the most common tension points among sedentary people surround the speech center: the neck, shoulders, throat, jaw and upper back.

Hoarseness and sore throat result from strain, and strain comes from tension in the muscles surrounding the larynx. So the next step toward effective projection of your voice without strain is remembering that voice is produced on exhalation and that it is pushed from the abdomen, not the throat. Mentally remind yourself as you speak that voice is a push from the gut.

Practice the breathing exercise for voice, which shows you how to inhale an adequate amount of air, then control the rate of exhalation, depending upon the volume you desire.

A warning: Pushing from the gut and having a relaxed throat are important, but the effect can be lost because of breathiness. Check your voice for breathiness and do the exercises following this section, if necessary. The breathy voice never projects. As stated earlier, it can also indicate growths on vocal cords or other physical problems, so check with a laryngologist.

Remember to open your mouth. Projecting literally means throwing your words out; your mouth must be wide open to do this. Clear, distinct articulation and drawing your words out with a sustained sound also will help your voice carry.

Finally, projecting your voice is closely related to your energy level. If you understand that you must project from your abdomen instead of from your throat, and if you really *want* to be heard—that is, if you're involved with your subject and you really want to make contact with your audience—you will generate enough energy in your voice to ensure that you are heard.

TO ELIMINATE BREATHINESS

1. Begin with your mouth open. Repeat *ho-ho-ho* and hold each vowel two seconds. Be aware of how you begin the sound. Avoid both harshness and breathiness. Repeat with *ha* and then *hu*.

2. Begin *hu*, then gradually change the vowel to *o* then to *ah*. Notice how your throat feels with each sound. Avoid strain and breathiness.

3. Practice economy of breath in the following:

eye	high
old	hold
at	hat
arm	harm
all	hall

4. Read the following, avoiding breathiness:

Peter Piper picked a peck of pickled peppers.
Blow bugle blow.

PROJECT THE VOICE

1. Repeat the following to someone beside you, someone ten feet away, someone in another room or at the back
of an auditorium. Keep your throat relaxed and your pitch
down.

No, hey, look out, don't do it.

2. Read the following for strength of tone and projection:

Beat on the buckskin, beat on the drums,
Hi! Hi! Hi! for the Thunderbird comes;
His eyes burn red with the blood of battle;
His wild wings roar in the medicine-rattle.
Thunderbird-god, while our spirits dance,
Tip with your lightning the warrior's lance;
On shafts of wind, with heads of flame,
Build for us arrows that torture and maim;
Ho! may our ironwood war-clubs crash
With a thunderbolt head and a lightning flash.
Hi! Hi! Hi! hear the Cut-throat's doom,
As our wild bells ring and our thunderdrums boom.
                    —"The Drummers Sing," from *Thunderdrums*,
                                              by Lew Sarett

Regional Accents

When people tell me they don't like their voice—that it is too
high, that they don't like its tone, or that they don't like their
accent—they are usually saying they don't like something
about themselves. For example, a woman who complains that
her voice is too soft or too high probably is struggling to become more assertive and authoritative.

A successful businesswoman who spoke with a pronounced Southern accent came to me intent on changing her accent because, she said, it made her sound like an empty-headed Southern belle. Her articulation was clear, she spoke with authority in her voice, and her accent was pleasant to the ear. I told her that the fact that she was *not* a silly Southern belle came across in everything about her: Her tone of voice, the precise, definite way she spoke, and the way she carried herself. My observations fell on deaf ears: She remained obsessed with a desire to get rid of her accent. I never did find out exactly what was going on inside her, but I believe that the intensity of her desire to lose her accent reflected some basic dissatisfaction with her own identity.

I rarely encourage people to get rid of regional accents unless they are difficult to understand, sloppy, careless or grating, as an excessively nasal accent can be. In situations like this, I encourage people to clean up their bad habits, but I don't encourage them to change their basic accent, because I believe that it usually is an integral part of who and what they are.

You should be concerned with improving your voice so that you can express the best of who and what you are—not change it.

Having said the above, I will qualify it with this: Some occupations, such as broadcasting or acting, require a standardized accent. If you have chosen an occupation that requires a "language wardrobe" different from your own, you will have to work to acquire a new one. Also, just as people are stereotyped because of their race, sex or physical appearance, some accents provoke stereotyped reactions. People often stereotype a person with a slow Southern drawl as dull or slow; a person with a fast, clipped Midwestern accent as a sharp wheeler-dealer; or a person with a BBC British accent as authoritative or aristocratic.

If you are an effective enough communicator and a strong enough person inside, you can override stereotyped reactions to your accent—just as a strong spoken image will override a negative visual image. But if you feel that stereotyped reactions to your accent are a real handicap, work to change it.

Voice coaches or speech therapists who specialize in accents often work with actors who wish to acquire specific accents for a play or film. So to find someone to help you change or modify your accent, check theater groups or university drama departments in your community. Or you might refer to the following books: Evangeline Machlin, *Speech for the Stage* (New York: Theatre Arts, 1966), which suggests specific records to listen to for speech improvement; J. Clifford Turner, editor, *Voice and Speech in the Theater* (New York: Drama Books, 1977); Dorothy Uris, *A Woman's Voice* (New York: Stein and Day, 1975). But understand that changing an accent you have grown up with will not be easy.

Improving Your Voice

We hear ourselves speak every day, but how little we actually listen to our own voices becomes obvious when we hear ourselves on tape and barely recognize ourselves. We do hear our voice slightly differently than others do, for physiological reasons. But the difference is minor. The main reason we don't recognize our voice is because we don't bother to listen to it. I am constantly amazed at how totally unaware of the sound of their own voices people can be. In my classes, persons with overt tremors or extremely high-pitched voices have expressed genuine surprise when I asked them if their voices had always been so shaky or high-pitched.

So self-awareness is the first step toward better voice production. Set a tape recorder beside your telephone and turn it on every time you speak for a week or two so that you will forget about it and be natural. Tape a speech you make to a large group.

Listen to the tapes when you have a quiet time. The first time you do this, don't try to analyze the quality of your voice; listen instead for uncertainty, the clarity of your articulation, the amount of upward inflection, your use of fillers such as "um," and "you know," and the overall feeling you get from listening to yourself. Does the voice you hear convey who you really think you are? If not, spend some time on it each day.

If you are bothered by constant huskiness, irritated throat or hoarseness, or chronic difficulty with breathing, or if you suffer from excessive nasality or denasality, you probably need specialized help beyond the scope of this book. A speech therapist or a laryngologist can help these kinds of problems.

Finally, remember that a good voice is not an end in itself. It is merely one means to your end, which is effective communication with your audience. The time to worry about the technicalities of voice production discussed in this chapter is *not* when you stand up to speak. When you stand up to speak, you should be thinking about using your energy to reach out and make contact with your audience. If you focus on that—and you've done the homework on your voice detailed in this chapter—your voice should take care of itself.

7

Listening to
Your Audience

An Ear for an Ear

Few of the people who come to me for help in becoming better speakers realize that they should be equally concerned with becoming better listeners. Effective communication is always two-way. Speaking without listening goes only one way.

As I have said, all my ideas revolve around my E.A.S.Y. concept. So if you understand why audience awareness is necessary to effective speaking, you will have no trouble understanding why an effective speaker must also be an effective listener. I could list a dozen reasons why a speaker *should* listen to his audience, but there are two purely pragmatic reasons why a speaker *must* listen. He must listen first to verify whether or not his message is being received—to see whether or not his audience is hearing and understanding his message.

Second, he must listen because, if he does not, his audience will not listen to him. Remember the performer described in Chapter 3? The performer's audience does not listen despite the fact that he seems to be a good speaker. He is energetic, knowl-edgeable, articulate and self-confident, but he talks at his au-dience instead of to them—a tacit message that their ideas are not important, that they are there simply as blotters to absorb his words. The audience tunes the performer out, although they may not consciously know why. The reason they do so is that they do not feel involved. For communication to be effective, both sender and receiver *must* feel involved in the exchange of information, ideas or feelings.

One of the most effective ways of making your audience feel involved is learning how to listen to them. Listening, really listening, is not easy. Contrary to popular thinking, listening is not an involuntary, physiological activity. Listening is an emo-tional activity.

Before I give specifics on how to listen to your audience, it is important to consider what listening is and how it functions.

Why Hearing Is Different from Listening

According to an Ohio University study, the average adult spends about 70 percent of his waking hours communicating in one form or another. Of that time, 9 percent is spent writing, 16 percent reading, 30 percent speaking, and 45 percent listen-ing. If we spend 45 percent of our communicating time listen-ing, it follows that it is important to know how to listen effec-tively. Most people assume that listening, unlike the learned skills of reading, writing and speaking, is a natural activity that anyone with unimpaired hearing can do with no effort. The reason this is not the case is partly physical, partly emotional.

Hearing *is* a natural, passive, involuntary activity. Anyone with a normally functioning ear and brain will involuntarily hear sounds of a certain intensity. But we do exercise control over the attention we pay to the sounds we hear. A person who lives beside a train track may say he never hears the trains. He does in fact hear them, but his nervous system is so accustomed to the sound that he can choose to tune it out and think about other things while his eardrum is vibrating from the sound of the train. Because he controls his thought processes, he can choose whether or not to listen.

We all know how easy it is to tune out sounds around us if we are thinking about something else. But even when we really try to listen to someone, we often find that our minds have wandered despite our good intentions and we have missed much of what he said.

The physiological reason our minds wander even when we try to listen is that the human brain is capable of processing words at a much higher speed than a person is able to speak. The average rate of speech for an American is about 125 words per minute; the human brain can process about 800 words per minute. While a speaker's words enter our brain at slow speed, we continue to think at high speed. So we have plenty of time to absorb the words the speaker is saying and think of other things at the same time. At first we can absorb everything the other person is saying, despite our private mental sidetracks. But unless we make a conscious effort to continue to listen, our private sidetracks tend to take over and before we know it we have missed some of his words because we were absorbed in our own thoughts.

The emotional reason listening is difficult concerns the nature of our private mental sidetracks. Curtailing them requires energy, discipline and concentration, and we must be motivated to exert an effort of that intensity. How highly motivated we are is determined by our attitude toward the speaker and his message—by how much we care about them. We cannot control the physiological fact that our minds are capable of absorbing words at a much higher speed than we can speak. But if we care enough about the information the speaker is conveying, or if he as a person is important enough to us, we will make the mental and emotional effort necessary to keep our minds clear of extraneous thoughts and really listen.

To become aware of how intently you must concentrate to really listen to another person, try the following exercise with one or several other persons.

Discuss any subject. Before each of you responds to another person, summarize in your own words and without notes what the other person has just said—to his satisfaction.

Be particular about the way other persons summarize what you have said. Don't let them off easily simply because you are impatient to continue the discussion.

Discussion Pointers

1. Did you find it difficult to listen to others in the group? If so, why?

2. Did you have trouble formulating your reply and listening at the same time? Why?

3. Were you satisfied that you conveyed to the others what you were trying to say?

4. How can you tell when other members of the group are listening and when they are only half listening?

5. Were certain members of the group listened to more closely than others? Why?

6. Based on this experience, can you list speakers' behaviors that make it easy to listen to them and behaviors that make it difficult to listen?

Learning to Say No When You Cannot Listen

Because genuine listening requires emotional involvement, it cannot be faked. A person pretending to listen gives himself away with nonverbal cues such as the look in his eyes or verbal cues such as the tone of his voice when he responds. Even over the telephone, when body language cannot be taken into account, most people can tell if the person on the other end of the line is listening intently or only half listening.

Because listening is impossible to fake, it is important to learn to tell people when you don't have the time or inclination to listen. If someone is in your office and the telephones are ringing and you're trying to meet a deadline, you should recognize the fact that you probably cannot listen effectively to the person at that time. Instead of giving him half your attention or faking attention, you should have the strength to say, "Look, Bob, I know what you have to say is very important, but as you can see there's no way I can give you my full attention right now. Why don't you come back in a couple of hours?" This kind of directness relates back to my concept of having the strength or self-esteem to let people know where you are. In my experience, people appreciate such honesty because it assures them that when you *do* listen, you will give them your full attention. Most people will respect the fact that you cannot always listen, and being told that you can't is much more reassuring than the uneasy feeling that you may have only half heard or partially understood them.

Learning to Listen to Your Audience

Understanding how much energy it takes for an audience just to listen to you should help you understand how much energy you must send out to them to motivate them to listen to you. Chapters 8 and 9 tell you how to make your audience sit up and listen to you. In this chapter, however, I am concerned with you, the speaker, learning how to make the mental and emotional effort to listen to your audience.

The first step toward effective listening is relaxation. If you're paralyzed by nervousness, the energy you should be focusing on your audience will become tension turned in on yourself. So first, use the relaxation techniques outlined in Chapter 5.

The next step is focusing visually on your audience. I don't believe in phony eye contact. But if you think of your audience as a group of individuals, each of whom you genuinely want to make contact with, and then establish eye contact with as many people as is physically possible, you have taken the first step toward "touching" your audience and letting them touch you. You have also begun to listen to them.

HOW YOUR AUDIENCE SPEAKS TO YOU

One reason people fear public speaking is because ritual dictates that the audience remain silent while the speaker delivers a prepared text. It's unnerving to speak to a silent audience, because you don't know what they are thinking.

The audience may not actually be speaking, but they are talking back in dozens of nonverbal ways. Experts estimate that 65 percent of our communication is nonverbal—or, in the current phrase, is transmitted through "body language." Every audience, whether it is one person or a thousand, communicates its reaction to a speaker in body language—through facial expressions, eye contact, body posture, gestures and movement.

So you listen to an audience with your eyes—by becoming sensitive to their nonverbal language. You listen with your ears too—to pick up disruptive noises in the room.

People generally assume that listening to a large audience is more difficult than to a small one, and that it must be done in a different way. In fact, there is little difference between listening to one person and to many. With a large audience you will not be able to see the details of every person in the room, but you will be able to see clearly the persons nearest you. And, if you listen, you'll be able to sense the feel of the room: whether it is calm or there are disruptive noises caused by restlessness— coughing, talking—or some element external to the audience, such as a noisy air conditioner or a record player in the next room. If your audience is not listening to you because of an external disturbance, it's up to you to deal with it. It may mean stopping and asking the audience if they can hear you above the air conditioner and, if not, asking someone to turn it off. Or, if you see people squinting or leaning forward, it may mean turning off a bright light, coming closer to the audience, or turning up the mike.

CARING ENOUGH TO LISTEN

So you listen to see if your audience is listening, and if for some reason they are not, you deal with the cause. You also listen so that your audience will listen to you. Nothing is more gratifying than another person's full attention. Really being listened to by another person is an implicit statement that he respects and cares about you and your feelings, thoughts and ideas. Nothing builds a person up, nothing reinforces his self-esteem, more than that. If you show your audience that you care enough about them to listen to them, they will sit up and listen to you. Your audience needs "strokes," just as you do, and if you take the trouble to stroke them, they will stroke you.

Large audiences are accustomed to being largely ignored by speakers. They assume that, no matter what they do, most speakers will drone on to the end of a prepared text. So they tune out and daydream, doodle or chat with their neighbor until the speaker has gone the predetermined distance. I have spoken to audiences like this on many occasions, and when I do, I take the trouble to gently zero in on the nappers and the chatterers and pull them back in. I say something like, "Are you with me?" or I simply pause and smile at the person in the fourth row with the faraway look in his eyes.

If it's a small group, side conversations often are important to the subject at hand, so it is important not to ignore them. If I were speaking at a business meeting of fifteen people or so, I might say to the three people talking among themselves, "That looks as if it might be important. Would you like to share it with the group?" Often they are discussing something I have said that needs clarification or elaboration, and the whole group benefits when they are encouraged to speak up.

When I "zero in" on people so that they will listen to me, I rarely do so in such a way that it embarrasses them—although I do not hesitate to single out a person who is being rude in some way, such as reading a newspaper or preventing other people from hearing me because he is talking. But usually, listening is a decidedly positive gesture of caring and respect toward an audience; it says you consider their attitudes and feelings important, too.

Active Listening

But the key to effective listening, no matter what the situation or the size of your audience, is "active listening."

The term "active listening" was first used in the fifties by psychotherapist Carl Rogers. It has been popularized by clinical psychologist Thomas Gordon in his book *L. E. T.—Leadership Effectiveness Training*.* Active listening is the most efficient, effective method I know to strip away the façades and

* Dr. Thomas Gordon, *L.E.T.—Leadership Effectiveness Training* (New York: Wyden Books, 1978).

barriers people erect and facilitate authentic communication. People muddy real communication by speaking in "code" to one another, saying one thing when in fact they mean another. For example: "How much longer is this meeting going to last?" The active listener "decodes" what the person is saying, viz: "You're pushed for time."

People speak in code because they don't want to reveal their real feelings. Active listening uncovers those feelings. Ironically, the person who had intentionally masked his real feelings is usually tremendously relieved at being really understood. To continue the example above:

"Yes. I have a plane to catch in an hour and a half, and there are several things I must do before I go to the airport."

When the active listener unmasks the other person's meaning he does not pass judgment or criticize what the other person has said. This is called the "blame-free statement." The blame-free statement serves two purposes: It uncovers the real meaning behind the words the person has used; and second, it reassures the person speaking that what he says will be fully understood and considered rationally and fairly rather than distorted, dismissed as stupid or silly, or worse, ignored while the other person expounds his own views.

The theory behind active listening is that you can achieve genuine understanding of another person's ideas and feelings only when you "walk in his shoes"—that is, psychologically "become" the other person and see the world through his eyes, instead of as an outside observer.

At this point, you probably are wondering how active listening can be applied to public speaking. Here's how: When I speak to a group, I listen actively from the moment I enter the room until the moment I leave. I try to imagine what it would be like if I were a successful salesman listening to a woman twenty years younger than myself telling me how to communicate more effectively; how I would feel if I were a policeman used to being an authority figure, listening to a woman telling me I needed to soften my image to establish better rapport with community groups.

When I said earlier that the speaker has to reach out of his private world to make contact with that of his audience, I was talking about active listening. At its most mundane, active listening can mean seeing people lean forward and squint at a diagram you are showing them and realizing that if you were looking through their eyes you probably wouldn't be able to see the diagram clearly. So you hold it closer to the audience, turn on a light, pass it around, or whatever.

When someone in an audience asks a question, active listening means listening for the meaning behind the words: listening to the tone of the voice, watching the face and body of the person asking the question, and if you have the background information, taking into consideration the attitudes and circumstances that might have prompted such a question.

The following examples illustrate how active listening opens up communication in a public-speaking or interview situation.

A well-known psychologist or attorney, being interviewed by the press:

Q.: Do you feel you can justify such high fees?
A.: (responding only to the words): My patients/clients don't seem to object.

OR

Well, I've spent years and years training for my position.

These responses would send out a message of defensiveness.

A.: (hostile): Do you feel *you* can justify the fee you get for making other people feel uncomfortable?

This response makes the audience side with the reporter and feel hostile toward the interviewee.

A.: (direct answer, responding only to words): No, I don't
feel I have to justify my fees.

This response might make the audience curious, frustrated or
angry, because they feel that the interviewee is hiding something.

A.: (active listening—responding to the facial expression
and tone of voice of the reporter): You feel my fees are
too high.

The reporter is now on the defensive and must give a logical
argument to back up his critical tone of voice. If he refuses to
answer, he is refusing to play by the same rules he sets for the
interviewee: i.e., openness. If the reporter is silent, this is his
responsibility, not the interviewee's.

Active listening in this situation has meant that the interviewee has neither been intimidated by the situation nor for-
gotten the reality. Active listening helps him to decode the
message the reporter is sending out and to deal with the reality,
which is: "You sure sounded and looked critical when you
asked that question."

A power company official has just completed a talk to a
group of consumers about a new nuclear plant and how it will
help meet their energy needs:

Q.: I don't give a damn about your big plant. I want to
know why my power bill keeps going up.
A.: (avoiding the issue): That's not my department. You'll
have to phone customer complaints.

This response would probably make the person asking the
question even angrier, because he would feel he is being ignored.

A.: (avoiding his responsibility as a spokesperson for the power company): I know what you mean. Mine's going up too.

This response would leave the questioner frustrated because no explanation or solution has been offered.

A.: (active listening): You sure are concerned.
Q.: You're right, I am concerned. If this keeps up, my electric bill will be higher than my mortgage.
A.: Well, I could go ahead and talk to you about why we need more money to build more plants to meet increased energy needs, but I don't think that will solve your problem. It seems to me you need to learn how to use energy more efficiently in your home so that you can try to lower your monthly bill.
Q.: Right.
A.: Did you know that we have people who will tour your home and tell you where you're wasting energy? After this talk, I'll give their number to anyone who wants it. I think they can help you with your problem.

By active listening, the power official has dealt with the person's problem squarely, instead of avoiding it or making the person even more angry by responding with hostility.

It is important to understand that if you work for a company or represent a group that has been under public attack, you *are* that company or group when you appear in public. The hostility in questions directed at you is not a personal attack; it is directed against the company. The obverse of this is that if you are able to establish yourself as a decent human being and you do make contact with the audience, the audience will leave with positive feelings about both you personally *and* your company. Hostility often arises from ignorance or misinformation.

A successful businesswoman has just completed a talk to a group of women interested in getting into management positions in business.

> Q.: Don't you think businessmen resent women who are assertive?
>
> A.: (responding only to the words): Oh, no—*my* experiences have all been very positive.

This response will not handle the woman's problem, which is resentment by men of her business manner.

> A.: (active listening—listening to the concern in her questioner's voice): You have a problem dealing with men.
>
> Q.: No, but I think some of the women I work with do.
>
> OR
>
> (in a tough, abrasive voice): Well, yes. The men who work with me resent me because I'm capable and assertive and refuse to put on a soft, sexy role.
>
> A.: (realizing from the woman's tone of voice that she doesn't understand the difference between assertiveness and aggressiveness): Do others in the audience have this problem?

Other members of the audience indicate they do, so the speaker breaks up the audience into small groups to discuss the difference between assertiveness and aggressiveness and how these influence other people's responses.

Active listening in this situation helped the speaker understand the audience's real needs and "where they were." Once she understood this, she was able to respond to their genuine need instead of talking about issues that might not be of immediate interest to them.

I am speaking to a group about effective public speaking.

Q.: Are you saying it's OK for me to put my hands in my pockets during a speech?

A.: (responding to the words): Yes, it's perfectly all right to put your hands in your pockets.

OR

(active listening, responding to the incredulous look on his face): You think that's a crazy idea, right?

Q.: (smiling): Well, I've taken a couple of speech courses and they both said I shouldn't stand like that. In fact you're telling me to ignore a lot of the things they taught me to do.

A.: (I now realize that he is struggling to decide whether he should believe me instead of the past authorities he has heard on the subject): Was I able to hold your attention even though I broke some of the rules your speech teachers taught you?

Q.: Yes.

A.: Are you willing to try a new way and see how it works for you?

Q.: Well, maybe. I suppose there's no really good reason why a speaker can't be natural.

Active listening is not an easy skill to learn. It requires effort and practice. You should use it first in one-to-one situations. For example:

Boss (to secretary, as she arrives at 9:15 A.M.): You're late.

Secretary: You're upset.

Boss: You're damn right I am. I've just wasted fifteen minutes on a call you should have handled.

Secretary: I understand you're under a lot of pressure to finish your report. You shouldn't have to waste

time doing my job. I'll make sure I'm here by
nine A.M. from now on.

To practice active listening, you must work with a partner.
A makes a statement dealing with a problem. *B* actively listens,
trying to zero in on *A*'s feelings. (This kind of exercise is much
more effective and meaningful if you talk about real—not hy-
pothetical—problems.) For example:

A: Dealing with employees sure is difficult today.
B: You've got a problem.
A: Yeh. This new manager needs a reason for everything I
   tell him to do.
B: It's frustrating to you.
A: That's right. After all, I'm the boss.
B: Explaining everything makes you feel as if you're giving
   up your authority.

Eventually, this kind of verbal exchange should lead *A* to ideas
for solutions.

An exercise in active listening such as this illustrates how
much energy it requires to really listen and understand another
person. When you speak, you are not simply asking your audience to sit back and passively absorb information. You are
asking them to give back to you as much energy as you are
giving out to them.

8

Winning Over Your Audience

Students sometimes tell me they feel nervous when they start to speak but relax once the audience starts to "warm up." My response to this is, "That's fine. But what if the audience never warms up?"

It's up to the speaker to warm up the audience, not the audience the speaker. I often compare speaker and audience to a puppeteer and a marionette: The puppeteer pulls the strings and the marionette responds. The speaker is in charge; he, not the audience, should determine what happens between them. Sure, the speaker has to be aware of the audience's needs and he must bend and adapt to meet those needs. But—and I cannot emphasize this strongly enough—he must remain in control of the situation; he must be the one who determines the outcome of the encounter.

But, you may be protesting, doesn't comparing speaker and audience to puppeteer and marionette suggest that the speaker is manipulating the audience, with all the negative connotations that implies? Not at all. The difference between manipulation and control lies in the motive. *Manipulate* means to manage with devious intent; *control* means exercising authority, directing the situation, taking charge.

The audience expects the speaker to be in control. They expect him to assume a role as teacher or leader. He is invited to speak because he is recognized as an authority in his field. When he stands up to speak, he physically assumes an authoritative posture; by remaining seated, the audience physically defers to him. The audience expects the speaker to take charge of the situation and deal with whatever happens while he is on his feet in front of the group.

Of course, the speaker must be sensitive to the audience's needs and concerns, but his real purpose is to teach the audience something. To do so, he must consider himself a winner. A little touch of cockiness helps. Remember what I said in Chapter 4 about why the effective speaker must have a positive self-image and let the audience know it? The necessity for the speaker to remain in control of the speaking situation is one more reason I object to false humility in a speaker. The audience is the student, the speaker the teacher: These are the natural dynamics of the speaking situation.

"Strokes"

I don't mean that the audience expects to sit quietly, hands folded, absorbing the speaker's information like sponges and accepting it as infallible truth. The audience wants the speaker to inform, enlighten, persuade or inspire, but they want the speaker to consider their ideas and opinions too. They want to be "stroked" by the speaker: They want him to care about their reactions, ideas and opinions, to respect them and to treat them as equals.

Because both speaker and audience are human, they both
want and need essentially the same thing. The speaker wants
and needs strokes, too, because the real reward of speaking is
the response of the audience. The speaker's need to be stroked
is what gives him the energy to reach out and make contact
with his audience. However, the speaker must strike a balance
between his desire for positive feedback and approval, and the
strength to state his views with conviction and authority and
maintain control while speaking.

How does the speaker control the speaking situation and at
the same time "warm up" the audience? He does it by genuinely wanting to make contact with his audience and by reaching out with his energy to do so. He does it by balancing sensitivity to his audience's needs and concerns and views, with
the strength to stand behind his own views. He does it by
going into every speaking situation expecting to establish common ground with his audience and working throughout the
speaking engagement to make that happen. All these techniques have been covered in earlier chapters.

Handling the Unexpected

But because speaking is a human situation, you can never pre-
dict exactly what is going to happen. You can prepare your
speech thoroughly, check and recheck details about the room
you will speak in, research the background, interests and opinions of your audience, but you can never be sure what will
happen. Someone else may speak on the same topic just before
you; someone in the audience may stand up five minutes into
your speech and say he disagrees with you; the audience's expectations may be totally different from yours; the slide projector may not work; or you may spill coffee on your jacket just
before you speak.

If you have read Chapter 5, you will know how to breathe

in order to relax in a moment of tension, you will know that being perfect doesn't contribute to authentic communication, and you will know what I mean by "dealing with the reality." All this should help you understand and accept the fact that, like any real-life situation, public speaking can never be totally predictable. If you accept this, you can learn to handle the situation just as you would if something similar happened while you were having a one-to-one conversation. Don't be afraid to be spontaneous—to say, "Boy, that sure has blown my introduction," or, "My speech teacher always said there'd be moments like this," or, "I don't think I could twist my tongue like that again if I tried."

How comfortably you handle unexpected situations involves your self-image. The more deeply you accept yourself as you are, the more comfortable you will be in any situation and the easier you will find it to maintain your cool. This doesn't mean "letting it all hang out." It does mean realistically accepting your strengths and weaknesses and being straight with your audience without apologizing. A film group asked me to give a talk about effective communication. Unknown to me, they advertised it in the local media as a workshop for TV directors and actors. When I arrived and met the audience, I knew immediately that many of them were expecting something quite different from my prepared talk. Some were models who thought they were going to learn something about acting on television, some were television and film directors, others were actors and scriptwriters.

So I started by saying: "Before I begin, I think it is important to deal with expectations—because I have a feeling that some of you came here with one expectation while I had another. What I do is help people speak more effectively. I have a lot of television experience, but I am not a professional TV director. I cannot give you tips on directing or acting. I plan to discuss how you come across to other people when you talk. If this is not something you're interested in, please feel free to leave. I won't be offended. But if you think my approach to speaking could help you, please stay and we'll try to make the evening worthwhile for all of us." I said this in a straight, unapologetic tone of voice. I realized that many members of the audience probably would not have come if they had understood in advance what I was going to talk about, but that didn't make me feel insecure or act apologetic. I knew what I could offer them and what I could not, and I simply stated it directly.

The Hostile Audience

"What if the audience doesn't like what I say?" "What if they disagree?" Or worse, "What if they're downright hostile?" These questions nag every speaker.

Active listening is the best way to deal with hostility, argumentativeness or honest disagreement. You must take into account the whole person, not only the words he says but the sound of his voice, his facial expression, and his body posture. If you simply respond to the words of the question or comment, you will not have dealt with the source of the hostility or disagreement. You have to "decode" the remark. For example: A businesswoman talks to a women's group about making it in the business world. One woman asks, "Don't you feel that it was easier for you to make it because you don't have children?" The businesswoman might respond, "Yes, but I know other women who do have children who have managed to get ahead in the business world." If she listened actively, she would respond, "You're finding it difficult to pursue a career because you have children."

The second answer responds to the whole message the woman sent out, instead of just to the words she used.

It is important to understand that the person who attacks you with a comment or question invariably is more interested in how you handle the response than in the response itself. A

reporter asked former Office of Management and Budget Director Bert Lance the following question: "This question comes in
two parts, Mr. Lance. The first is: Is it true that on your recent
trip to Europe you went as a personal envoy of President Carter
and met on his behalf with various heads of state? If so, whom
did you meet with? And the second part of this question is:
Now that you're a journalist, how do you feel about people who
don't return your phone calls?"

With a disarming smile, Lance replied, "I'll respond to the
second part of your question first. People *do* return my phone
calls. And if the phone call you placed to me last week was to
ask the first part of your question, I wasn't going to respond to
it then and I'm not going to respond to it now." The reporter's
underlying question was "Why didn't you return my phone
call last week?" By active listening, Lance uncovered what the
reporter was thinking. And the reporter was so impressed with
the style of his reply, he let the fact that he did not answer his
question pass by the board.

When people direct hostile questions at a speaker, they almost never are being straight with him. Yet, strange as it may
sound, no matter what kind of nasty game the person is playing, he invariably is relieved when the speaker penetrates his
façade and exposes what he is really thinking. No matter what
the situation, there is tremendous relief in being really understood by another person. If a colleague stands up at a business
meeting waving a report you wrote and says, "This is really
lousy," your reflex response might be to start defending the
report. The active listener would say, "You're really upset."
Then he would find out the reason the person didn't like the
report, e.g.: "You bet I am. There wasn't one mention of our
whole department in this thing."

Because active listening helps keep you emotionally detached from a verbal attack, it helps you maintain your cool. It
allows you to deflect an attack rather than counterattacking or

becoming defensive. If someone aims a sarcastic comment at you, the reflex reaction often is to fight fire with fire and return an equally caustic remark. The problem with this is that you have not dealt with the reality, which is the meaning underlying the remark. (Sarcasm usually is a cover-up for something a person will not say directly). Also, it ignites a fight, and when two people fight, one person usually wins and the other loses. If the speaker wins, the other members of the audience will tend to sympathize or feel sorry for the loser, and if the speaker loses, he will have lost control of the situation.

It should go without saying that there is no place for sarcasm initiated by the speaker. Sarcasm is a cowardly way of sidestepping what you really mean; is neither direct nor authentic; and has no place in a situation where people are trying to communicate. Sarcasm indicates lack of respect for your audience, and you cannot hope to communicate if you are condescending.

Another way to deflect hostility is for the speaker to openly acknowledge the reality but choose to ignore it. I saw an excellent example of this when a colleague of mine was asked a question in a sarcastic tone of voice. He looked at the person, smiled, and said, "That sounds like a trap to me." He then moved on to the next question.

Applying active listening effectively in confrontations is a skill that requires practice. But if you practice active listening in relaxed, one-to-one situations, as suggested in Chapter 7, you will find it much easier to apply when you have been verbally attacked and are under stress.

Questions and Answers

The question-and-answer period is a very important part of every speech. You cannot be sure you are getting your message across to your audience until you get feedback from them and find out what is on their minds. You can listen to your audience with your eyes, but the only sure way of knowing what they are thinking, whether they understand, agree or disagree, is through a question-and-answer dialogue.

When I'm told I have thirty minutes to fill, I don't prepare a thirty-minute talk, although I always have extra material prepared in case the group doesn't have many questions. It varies according to the situation but normally I prepare a fifteen-minute talk and leave the other fifteen minutes for questions. Consider the specifics of each speaking situation and, working from your knowledge of the audience's needs and concerns, decide how long you should set aside for questions. Sometimes you can dispense with a prepared text entirely and simply hold a question-and-answer session, although you should never go into a speaking situation with nothing prepared to say.

The effectiveness of a question-and-answer period depends to some degree on the size of the audience. It is impractical to invite questions from an audience of 1,000 people. If you anticipate that your audience will be about 200 people or more, it can be helpful to have a representative selection of persons in the audience submit written questions before you begin to talk. If the audience is more than 50 people, microphones interspersed throughout the room can assure that questions will be heard clearly by everyone. When you receive a question, repeat or paraphrase it before answering, to ensure that you have understood it correctly and that everyone in the audience has heard it.

Inexperienced speakers often dread the question-and-answer period even more than the speech itself. They're afraid no one will ask any questions and they'll be left standing dumbly in front of a silent audience. Or they feel that preparing a speech is dealing with a known quantity, while dealing with questions enters the realm of the unknown, because you can never anticipate exactly what someone is going to throw at you.

They're afraid that someone will ask a question they can't answer or argue with something they've said, that they'll be "shot down," look stupid, or be at a loss for words.

How do you deal with fears like this?

First, what if no one asks any questions? Understand that asking a question entails risk. The attention of the audience will be focused on the person asking the question; this is enough to make many people so uncomfortable and self-conscious that they never take the risk of asking a question. A person who asks a question also runs the risk of people thinking he has asked something stupid or irrelevant, something that has already been adequately explained by the speaker, or something that others will think he should already know because of his position. I realized this early in my speaking career when I was talking to the heads of a number of public relations firms. Damned if they were going to risk appearing ignorant or ill-informed in front of their professional competitors!

So if no one asks a question immediately, don't assume you haven't sparked any interest in the audience. Invite questions by saying, "What are your questions?" instead of "Are there any questions?" If no one responds right away, be prepared to hold the silence for a few minutes and wait. You can deal with the reality by saying, "Well, we have ten minutes left and I can continue, but I'd rather wait a minute and see what your specific concerns are." Or you can say, "OK, if there are no questions right now, let me mention a question I am often asked."

If you've done your homework and have found out as much as possible about the group before you speak, you can break the ice by suggesting topics the group might have questions about. For instance, "It seems to me that people such as you, involved in X, might be concerned about Y. Does anyone have any specific questions about Y?" If you see someone in the audience who seems comfortable and relaxed and really looks as if he's with you, you could say in an unpressuring way,

"Bill, do you have any feelings about that?" But you have to treat the person with a lot of consideration and not be upset or lose your equilibrium if you don't get an answer.

If you have held the silence for a fair length of time and no one speaks up, you can say, "Well, if you have no questions, I'll continue." I suggest this only as a last resort, because when you do it you give up interaction with the audience, and that is what speaking is all about.

Your own comfort with silence and the warmth you have projected to the audience during your speech greatly influence the question-and-answer period. If you've been detached throughout your speech, don't expect your audience to get involved all of a sudden.

It is natural to let down and relax a little after delivering a speech, so you probably will find you are more relaxed during the question-and-answer period than you were while delivering the prepared part of your speech.

If you thoroughly prepare your speech and are familiar and comfortable with your subject, you should be confident that you will be able to handle questions adequately.

The worst thing that can happen in a question-and-answer period is that someone will ask you something you don't know or will say he disagrees with you. This brings us back to the unrealistic desire to be perfect. You don't have to know everything. You don't have to be perfect. If you have the strength to admit you don't know something—without apologies—no one is going to criticize you. Often you'll be able to suggest a source that might have the information. For example, if you're talking about women in the work force and someone asks you the percentage increase over the last ten years of married women working full-time, you can say you don't have the exact figures in your head but the Department of Labor or the National Organization for Women probably could give him the figures.

If someone disagrees with you, you can apply the active listening techniques I have outlined to find out whether the person genuinely disagrees and is being straight with you, or is masking feelings about something else. An honest difference of opinion is nothing to be afraid of. One reason you are there is to get people thinking about your subject, and there is no more effective way to make people think than to let them hear two opposing opinions. It is important to confine your criticism to the person's ideas, not the person, even if he makes a personal attack on you. As I said above, active listening will help you keep from getting emotionally involved.

After I gave a talk on why I seldom recommend reading a manuscript speech, a member of the audience said, "Don't you think most people feel more comfortable with a manuscript speech?" I active-listened and answered, "You're more comfortable with one." He replied, "Yes, I really am. I just don't think I could get up and speak extemporaneously." "If you're really uncomfortable speaking extemporaneously, go ahead and use a manuscript speech," I said. "But I would like you to try portions extemporaneously. See how that works."

His question was less an attack than an expression of genuine doubt. By dealing with his real problem—fear of speaking without a manuscript—I was able to offer him a possible solution.

Embarrassing, biased, irrelevant or otherwise inappropriate questions may be thrown at you. Someone may ask about your personal life, make a bigoted remark about someone's race, religion or sex, or broach a subject the organization you work for does not wish to discuss publicly.

In each of these instances, you can politely refuse to answer. For example:

Q.: What does your husband think of you traveling?
OR
Does it bother your wife that you work with so many attractive women?
A.: You'd have to ask my husband/wife.

Q.: How much money do you make?
A.: That's a matter of public record. Anyone interested can read our annual report.

A journalist interviewing a Catholic gynecologist involved in the antiabortion Right to Life movement asked, "Do you think it's right that your religion affects the way you practice medicine?" The doctor replied in a sarcastic tone, "Does the fact that you're Jewish affect *your* attitude toward birth control?" She replied, "That's not relevant to what we're discussing, which is your involvement in the antiabortion movement."

If it is obvious to the rest of the audience as well as yourself that the question is inappropriate, you can deftly deflect the question back to an appropriate related subject or to the subject at hand. Shortly after Jimmy Carter's infamous *Playboy* magazine interview was published, during the 1976 presidential campaign, Rosalynn Carter used this technique effectively when a reporter asked her if she lusted in her heart after men. Without flinching, she replied evenly, "I believe in equal rights for men and women." Her tone of voice made it clear that she had nothing more to say about the matter and that she considered the subject closed. But she avoided losing dignity or credibility by giving a direct yes or no answer, or creating a confrontation by refusing to answer.

I never recommend dishonesty, and in most cases I believe that a speaker should be as direct as possible. If your company cannot discuss X publicly, say so. It may be unfavorable publicity for your company in the short run, but in the long run it is infinitely better than being exposed to charges of covering up, telling half-truths, or lying. For example:

Q.: Did your company really bribe officials in Iran?
A.: Since our investigation is not complete, I can't discuss that at the present time.

If he is pressed by the questioner, he could reply:

> A.: Come on, Joe, you don't want me to lose my job, do
> you?
>
> OR
>
> You know I can't discuss that at this time.

When addressing a group of black college students about opportunities in journalism, a correspondent for a national magazine was asked why such a low percentage of blacks were correspondents for the magazine. She replied, "Until recently, very few blacks have applied for a job with this magazine because they didn't identify with the world it described. Also, blacks graduating from college are drawn more often to TV journalism because the rewards come faster and it is more ego-gratifying."

This was only part of the truth. The other part was that the magazine found it difficult to find qualified blacks with the necessary writing skills because they had not taken the courses they needed.

I believe that those students needed to understand why blacks were underrepresented in print journalism so that they would have a realistic idea of what they had to do to make it themselves.

Credibility with Your Audience

If you aren't straight with your audience, you probably will jeopardize your credibility. Because even when our words sound convincing, our bodies give us away in dozens of ways. In his recent book *Manwatching,* Desmond Morris writes that "whole-body lying" is much more difficult than lying with words or facial expressions. A person who is lying or for some reason is uncomfortable with what he is saying, Morris goes on, will suppress the number of hand gestures he would naturally use to emphasize points, and often will touch his nose or cover his mouth with one of his hands. Studies consistently find that words convey very little of our meaning. One study comparing the relative importance of words, tone of voice, and facial expression, concludes that facial expression conveys 55 percent of meaning, tone of voice 38 percent, and words only 7 percent. So unless you are prepared to spend a lot of time perfecting "whole-body lying," you are best off telling the truth and telling it straight if you want your audience to believe you.

I'm not saying your audience will be skilled in interpreting body language. But when you are not speaking forthrightly, your body registers your evasiveness by an increase in tension, and people do subconsciously pick up and interpret nuances of tension in a person's body. If your body doesn't jibe with your words, your audience will sense you are hiding something, although they may not be able to pinpoint exactly how they know this.

Other pointers about credibility: You wouldn't be asked to speak if you weren't recognized as a spokesperson for your field, so don't footnote your speech excessively. John F. Kennedy may have said it before you, and it's fine to use the odd quote, but if you lard your speech with references to outside authorities, you will diminish your credibility as an authority in your own right.

And there is no substitute for speaking with energy, giving your audience direct eye contact, and using your own words instead of reading from a manuscript. (I will say more about this in the next chapter, when I talk about manuscript speeches.) How can you expect people to believe you are convinced of what you are saying if you have to read it to them? Speaking extemporaneously does not mean speaking impromptu or entirely without notes. It means taking the time to prepare your speech properly and become familiar with your subject so that your knowledge is an integral part of you. Then, when you speak it, you will say it in your own words, you will say it spontaneously, and it will be unmistakably authentic.

That's credibility.

9

Preparing and Delivering Your Speech

Most people begin speaking in public more out of necessity or obligation than genuine desire. Many consent to speak only when their jobs demand it.

Yet there are many reasons to go out of your way to speak.

First, for your psyche. Speaking to a group of people is an exercise in assertion with the inherent rewards of assertive behavior. Assertiveness builds self-confidence, and also, there is no confidence-builder more powerful than positive, immediate response from a group of people. Applause is tangible recognition for a job well done. It is applause—the positive, immediate response to a person's effort to communicate—that hooks all performers and keeps them coming back for more. It hooks speakers too. A letter of praise, a favorable article in a magazine or newspaper, a promotion—none of these is as immediately tangible and ego-gratifying as applause for a speech.

Speaking is also an exercise in power. The "high" that

hooks speakers, and all performers, doesn't come only from the applause; it also comes from the sense of power of being in control of an audience. It's heady stuff and once you've experienced it you'll keep coming back for more.

Second, on a purely pragmatic level, speaking will hurry you along the road toward recognition, prominence and promotion. The silent person is seldom recognized. The personal exposure you get by speaking is one of the most effective ways to become known as an authority in your field. Writing or being written about will never give you the kind of recognition that speaking will. To be trite, people need a face to remember a name.

The higher you rise in your organization, the more prominent you become in your field, the more you will be called upon to act as a spokesperson. And, all things being equal, the more vocal you are, the more willing you are to speak out, the faster you will advance.

Face-to-Face Contact

A speech without an audience is like a story without a reader. It is the flesh-and-blood confrontation, the face-to-face contact that sets a speech apart from other forms of social communication. Every speech serves two purposes: to give the audience the information they want, and to convince them that John Smith is an expert in photography, that the People's Bank cares about the community, that the Widget Corporation makes better widgets than its competitors. The personality of the speaker is always involved. As I said in Chapter 3, the flavor of you is inseparable from every speech you make. The face-to-face contact makes speech an ideal medium for involving people's emotions, for influencing their ideas, for persuading them to act in a certain way.

In short, a speech is an ideal selling medium, whether you are selling yourself, your expertise, your organization's goodwill or your company's product. The key is the personal contact. Credibility comes from you, as well as from the idea or product you are trying to sell. Other persons or organizations promote ideas or products similar to yours. You sell your personal viewpoint or product by selling yourself, and a speech is the ideal medium to accomplish this. One-dollar to multi-million-dollar decisions are often made as much on the strength of the salesperson's image as on the strengths of the product or service.

An insurance salesman talks to a Kiwanis Club about the importance of disability insurance. What he really is doing is building public confidence in him and his company as sellers of disability insurance. His speech may not reach as wide an audience as a paid advertisement, but its effect will be much more incisive.

Making Something Happen

The purpose of every speech, whether it is a eulogy or a call to arms, is to make something happen, and it is worthless unless it moves the audience in some way. Every speech should stimulate and entertain, not in the humorous sense but in the sense that it should make its subject as interesting and exciting as possible. Unless you are the exceptional person who handles humor well, leave professional entertainment to the experts.

Academic texts about speaking often devote pages to definitions of different kinds of speeches, but most can be labeled informative or persuasive or some combination of the two. An informative speech is simply a sharing of information—an unbiased report of a situation. A persuasive speech states a definite opinion the speaker wants the audience to share.

Preparing Your Speech

Preparation begins the moment you are asked to speak. Find out as much as you can about your audience, the occasion, the place and the conditions under which you will speak. Ask what brings the audience together in the first place. Is their common bond the organization they work for, the school they attend, their occupation, the neighborhood they live in, a hobby, civic interest, a political party? Will they attend by choice or obligation? What is the age range, the male/female ratio, the racial mix, the educational background, the economic status of the group? How much do they know about your subject? Are they interested in an overview or a specific aspect, or do they want your viewpoint on an issue? How much time will you have? Where will you be on the program: the first speaker, when the audience is fresh, or at the end of a long day? Will the audience have been drinking? This is also the time to discuss fee if you are a paid speaker.

Enter the answers to these questions on a form similar to the one on the following pages, and keep it on file.

Once these questions are answered, your first decision is whether or not to accept the invitation. Give yourself time to think about it; tell the person who contacts you that you'll give a definite answer within a few days. Although I believe people should be receptive to every opportunity to speak, there are times when you should refuse. Don't agree to speak on a topic you know little about or have little interest in, or when you will be given five minutes and need twenty. If you are to speak about a serious topic, don't hesitate to refuse if your audience will have just come from a two-hour cocktail party.

YOUR APPROACH

Learning as much as you can about your audience and their expectations of you will help you decide on the approach you will take to your subject. Never let your host decide on an exact title or approach to your topic. If your specialty is open classroom education and a women's club asks you to speak about it, find out why they are interested: Is there an open classroom school in their neighborhood that they are considering sending their children to? Is a local school changing from a traditional to an open classroom method? Will you be one of a series of educators talking about different approaches to education? Do they as a group oppose the open classroom method? Find out as much as possible about where they are and what they are interested in. Then *you* decide how you will approach the subject and, if they request it, give them a title for your talk.

This relates back to audience awareness and strength. Be sensitive to your audience's needs and desires; but stand firm on who and what you are. Tailor your subject to the interests of your audience, but don't let your awareness of their point of view dilute what you really want to say. Strike a balance between the questions "What do I want to say?" and "What is relevant to the audience?"

Date of contact_____
Date of seminar_____

PROPOSAL FOR SPEECH, SEMINAR, WORKSHOP

1. For_____
   _____
2. Initial contact _____

Address _____
Phone _____
3. Working contact_____
   Address _____
   Phone_____
4. Date of Speech_____ Time_____
5. Location_____
6. Directions _____
   _____
   _____
7. Number of People _____
8. Details of location:
   a/ Description of room_____
   _____
   b/ Microphone_____
   c/ Lectern _____
   d/ Audiovisual_____
   e/ Miscellaneous _____
   _____
9. Title of presentation _____
10. Content (main ideas) _____
    _____
    _____
    _____
11. Speaker will supply_____
    _____
    _____
    _____
12. They will supply _____
    _____
    _____
    _____
13. Fee _____
14. Letter of confirmation sent on _____

15. Brief introduction sent on _____
16. Further comments _____

_____
_____
_____

CHECKPOINTS

Once you have agreed to speak, you need answers to still more questions. The following list is intended as a guideline only. Check any other details that are relevant to your particular talk. The important thing is to check and recheck even the smallest detail.

1. *Getting there:* Get detailed directions to the place you will speak. If you're responsible for your own transportation, how long will it take you? Will you be in rush-hour traffic? Where can you park? If you are speaking in another city and someone is meeting you at the airport or at your hotel, get precise details.

2. *The place:* How large is the room? What shape is it? How will the audience be seated (rows, semicircle, at tables)? Will you be speaking on a stage, a platform or directly in front of your audience? Will there be a lectern?

3. *Acoustics:* Will a microphone be necessary? If so, what kind of microphone will be provided (standing microphone, desk microphone attached to a lectern, or neck microphone that will allow you to move freely)? If you prefer one to another, request it.

4. *Equipment:* If you're going to use audiovisual aids, be sure there is a suitable place to put them and that they will be clearly visible to everyone in the audience. If your equipment needs to be plugged in, ask about electrical outlets.

5. *The program:* Who will introduce you? Give your host

biographical details, or if you prefer, write your own introduction.

REMEMBER: CHECK AND RECHECK!

Don't assume anything. Ask for every single thing you'll need. The less you know about the group, the more important it is to get everything confirmed in writing.

If you're using visual aids, make a personal checklist for yourself so that you won't find yourself in front of a flip chart without a marker or with a slide projector without an extension cord. Hosts often overlook details, so take personal responsibility for everything you will need. For example, don't assume your host will remember to provide a glass of water for you: Ask for one. Don't assume you will have a place to put your notes: Ask whether there will be a lectern or table. I once found myself behind an expensive Plexiglas lectern that was beautiful to look at but supremely impractical. The light bounced off it, producing a glare for the audience, and the angle was such that my notes slid off and it was impossible to balance a glass of water on it.

Of course, meticulously checking details doesn't ensure that everything you need will be in place. But it does reduce the chances of slip-ups.

TALK YOUR SPEECH

The best way to begin preparing a speech is by talking your ideas into a tape recorder, then transcribing and editing them. Basically I'm against writing out a speech word for word, because most people take the conversational tone out of their words when they write. Also, when something is written out word for word, people tend to memorize the words rather than familiarizing themselves with the ideas.

I practice talking a speech first from a detailed outline, then from a few big ideas on cue cards. Experiment to see what suits you best. Notes are meant to prod your memory, so use whatever words or phrases you need to jog your mind. If one word on a cue card is enough, use one word on a cue card. If you need a detailed outline, use a detailed outline.

One word of caution: Most people make too many notes. Then, when they look down, all they see is a jumble. So be sure the writing or printing is large enough and clear enough for you to understand it at a glance. Three-by-five-inch cards are practical. Either number them or punch holes in them and put them in a binder so that you'll be sure not to get them out of order.

A speech by definition is spoken, so the way to practice it is to speak it. Talk it and talk it again. A friend, colleague or spouse can critique it for you, or you can use a tape recorder to analyze it yourself.

USE BIG IDEAS

Before you begin preparing the body of your speech, you must have a crystal-clear idea of its purpose. If you cannot express in a single sentence exactly what you want your speech to accomplish, your idea is too fuzzy.

Remember the line, "Sorry about the long letter—I would have written a short one, but I didn't have the time"? It takes time, concentration and effort to reduce your ideas and knowledge about a subject to a few clear, easily grasped points. People cannot absorb nearly as much oral information as they can written. If the audience needs more details about your subject, give it to them in writing after your speech.

But use your speech to impress your "big ideas" on the audience. Big ideas are the major points you want to emphasize. They should act as magnets for all the little ones. If the details are structured around a few clearly stated big ideas, the organization of the whole speech will fall into place.

The big idea in this book is my concept of E.A.S.Y. If all you remember when you close this book is the meaning of E.A.S.Y., I will have accomplished my purpose, because all my little ideas are subordinate to it. After a speech the audience should be able to say, "The speaker made this [or these] major point[s]." If they only remember your general topic—that you talked about Company X's marketing policy, for example, you've failed. They should be able to remember the three specific methods Company X uses to market its products.

As a rule of thumb, one big idea is enough for a five-minute talk; no more than two or three should be included in a twenty-minute talk. For example, in a twenty-minute talk about estate planning, you could cover three big questions: What do you own? Who do you want to have it? How can you will it with the least possible tax?

BE SPECIFIC, CONCRETE, VISUAL

Talking in big ideas doesn't mean talking in generalities. The language of a speech should be specific, concrete and visual; and whenever possible, you should illustrate a general idea with a specific, human example. If your big idea is that X million Americans are functionally illiterate, illustrate this with the poignant story of thirty-five-year-old Stacey Jones, who has lost job after job and is living on welfare because she can't read.

No matter how intelligent your audience or how specialized their knowledge, they cannot absorb nearly as many abstract or complex ideas by ear as they can visually. When people read, they pause, ponder and reread. When they listen, they have only one chance to grasp the meaning. So use simple, forthright, direct and visual language, no matter what the educational level or technical expertise of your audience. If you load a speech with jargon, complex words and complicated sentence structures, you are abusing speech as a medium of communication. Obtuse or flowery language calls attention to itself rather than to the message. Your purpose is to get your message across. Subordinate style to substance. Make every sentence, every phrase, every word, pass the same test: "Does it convey my idea as directly, as simply, and as graphically as possible? Will the audience instantly understand what I am saying or will they have to stop and rephrase it, think about it, or wonder what I mean?"

I'm not saying you should talk to your audience as if they had the comprehension of third-graders. I'm saying be direct to the point of bluntness. For example:

> The city has a majority black population, a black mayor, and a city council that is half black. Blacks are enjoying new economic freedom, new political clout and new positions of leadership, and it's all quite scary to some whites.

Use metaphors only if they are graphic and the analogy is not labored. A metaphor that works:

> Our metropolitan region needs a transfusion—one to head off the crippling anemia of stagnant growth, empty office space, a shrinking tax base, and citizen apathy. But we seem to be unable to agree on where we should get the needle or who should hold it.

The emphasis of this book is on your spoken image, not the technicalities of speech writing. If you feel you need more help with the latter, the following books may be useful: Roger P. Wilcox, *Oral Reporting in Business and Industry* (Englewood Cliffs, N.J.: Prentice-Hall, 1967); John Ott, *How to Write and Deliver a Speech* (New York: Trident Press, a division of Simon and Schuster, 1970).

PULLING YOUR AUDIENCE IN

Begin your speech with a statement that makes your audience sit up and listen, and establishes you as a human being.

First impressions resist change. If you lose your audience in the first couple of minutes, chances are you'll have lost them for the entire speech. If you establish rapport at the outset, chances are your audience will stay with you. So if your audience is with you when you begin your speech and your mind goes blank five minutes later, their reaction will be "That's fine, Joe. We're enjoying this. We're with you. Take a moment to get your thoughts together and then we'll go on."

Speakers often begin by stating or rephrasing the title of their speech, or by giving a brief summary of what they're going to say. An opening like this doesn't give the audience any compelling reason to listen.

Every audience is asking the question, if only subconsciously, "Why should I listen?" No matter how much your audience needs your information—even if their getting a job or a promotion depends on absorbing it—it is your responsibility to hook them at the outset.

You don't have to be especially imaginative or creative to think of a way to pull your audience in with your opening remarks. All it takes is a little thought. A woman raising funds for the Cancer Society began a speech to a group of twenty-eight people like this: "In America we use the word equality a lot. In spite of that fact, all of us in this room are not equal. Some of us are more equal than the rest because one in four of us will be struck with cancer." She didn't do anything unusually creative. All she did was take a statistic—one in four Americans contracts cancer—and personalize it for the audience. But you'd better believe that that audience sat up and listened.

A bank president speaking at a dinner honoring employees

with fifteen or more years of service to the bank began his speech like this:

> Some years back, Barbra Streisand made a song called "People" famous. As I look out over this audience tonight, the words to that song echo through my mind: "People, people who need people, are the luckiest people in the world."
>
> If that song is true, then I am among the very luckiest people in the world. And the shareholders of this bank are among the luckiest. Because from my vantage point, it is impossible not to recognize that our need for people, people like you, is absolute.
>
> Without you, the doors would not open. There would be no customers. No profits for shareholders. There would be no bank.
>
> Our need for people like you is magnified by the nature of our business. Some say it is a business of selling money. I don't think so. It's a business of hopes and dreams and security.
>
> And hopes and dreams are not sold by advertising or machines. They are sold by people.
>
> That is why we are here tonight. To acknowledge in a small way our debt to you . . . to say "Thank you for continuing to serve when you are needed."

The main purpose of his speech was to reinforce warm feelings between him and his employees, to communicate to them that he cared about them and that they were important to him. The reference to Barbra Streisand's song pulled the audience in and at the same time established him as a human being.

The opening also should be relevant to the rest of the speech. One reason I don't advise using a joke to start is that it usually has nothing to do with what follows. For another reason, most of us are not entertainers and don't tell jokes particularly well. And the audience may have heard the joke. So open with one only if it is fresh, you tell it well, and it ties in to the rest of your speech. Because the opening is crucial to involving your audience, and because most people are at their most nervous when they first stand up to speak, I suggest preparing a choreographed opening and rehearsing it until it is perfect. If you deliver an orchestrated opening without reference to notes, give the audience lots of eye contact, and carry it off without a hitch, you will involve your audience and bolster your confidence at the same time.

OPENERS

Bearing in mind the guidelines above, consider these suggestions for opening:

1. *A dramatic or startling statement:* This opening jolts the audience into sitting up and listening. For example, "A woman's place is in the home," to a feminist group, will make them bristle but it will also make them listen.

Beginning this way is risky, because you may alienate your audience. It also requires strength, because the statement must be delivered with energy and allowed to stand on its own, not run on into the next statement. If the speaker says, "A woman's place is in the home—of course, we all know this is ridiculous," he loses the entire impact of the opening. Effective use of the pause is important when a strong statement is used to begin a speech.

2. *Eliciting a unison reaction from the audience:* Involve the audience and evoke a response from them by asking a direct question, a rhetorical question ("Would you like to know how and when you'll die?"), or making a statement such as "Raise your hand if you want better public schools in the

county." The effectiveness of this kind of opening also depends on the pause and involves risk, because the audience may not respond as you expect they will. Someone may shout out a negative answer. So if you choose this kind of opening, be prepared with a rejoinder, no matter how the audience responds.

3. *Reference to a recent or well-known event:* If you are talking about the need for stricter enforcement of construction regulations, you could start your speech by quoting a recent newspaper headline: "Elevated highway collapses killing fifty-four people." If your subject is corruption in city government, you could begin with a headline referring to a scandal in the police department. Choose an event that most members of the audience will remember vividly; this will involve them because they will conjure up their own visual images or impressions of it.

4. *Personal experience:* Well-told, an amusing personal experience can establish rapport with the audience by making them smile, while at the same time making the speaker a person. Unless you handle humor well, stick to a personal experience that is sincere, reveals something of you, and is relevant to the subject at hand. Use it only if it has a definite purpose. If you're on an ego trip, your audience will tune out.

5. *Anecdote or illustration:* If you're arguing that social security benefits ought to be increased, a case history of a sixty-eight-year-old widow living on social security will get your point across much more effectively than statistics about inflation and the rising cost of living. Once again, the anecdote must be pertinent.

6. *Quotation:* A quotation by definition lacks spontaneity. So, to be effective, it must be spoken with a lot of energy. It should be brief and to the point and directly relevant to the topic. A banker addressing the industry's serious

problems during a recession began a speech to a convention of bank officers by quoting Franklin D. Roosevelt's famous statement, "The only thing we have to fear is fear itself." He then went on to suggest positive steps the banking industry could take to deal with its problems. The quotation worked because it was brief, to the point, relevant and familiar to the audience. Unless you're a thespian, you probably will lose your audience if you begin by reciting a dozen lines from Shakespeare.

7. *Definition:* Dictionary definitions tend to be dry, so I don't recommend using a definition to open a speech unless it is dramatic and tells the audience something new—the more startling the better. Again, it must lead in to the subject of the speech.

8. *Reference to a previous speaker:* Use this only if it is spontaneous and an ideal lead-in to your speech.

9. *Statement of central idea of speech:* As I said above, an introduction should not tell your audience what you are going to say; it should make the audience sit up and listen. So use this opening only if it is a strong statement. For example, in a speech exposing filthy kitchen conditions in city restaurants, you could begin: "Not a single restaurant in the center of this city serves food fit for human consumption."

10. *Visual aid:* If you're talking about hunger in India and you have a slide that graphically illustrates the physical condition of a starving child, it will make your audience sit up and listen. But in most cases, using a visual aid is a weak way to start a speech because the focus is on the aid rather than the speaker.

11. *Establishing common ground with the audience:* This beginning both involves the audience and establishes the speaker as a person. For example: "We all know the saying 'Nothing is certain but death and taxes.' We all try to pay as

few taxes as possible, and some people think we CPA's have cornered the market on tax breaks. That's not necessarily true, but here are some tips on filling out your tax return that may save you some money."

12. *Analogy:* Analogy is effective if the comparison is valid and not labored. A politician speaking to a group of financial executives began:

> The first battle of Atlanta, in 1864, was one of the turning points of the War Between the States. The city was burned to the ground; Sherman marched to the sea and broke the back of the Confederacy.
>
> What is not widely known is that it didn't have to happen. Historians tell us the city had well-built defense works and could have withstood a long siege. This would have meant failure for the Union army that could have weakened their resolve and even jeopardized President Lincoln's chances for re-election.
>
> Now I don't know if that would have been good or bad. Certainly it would have been good for this city not to have been destroyed.
>
> What I *am* concerned about is the *second* battle of Atlanta, for which troops are now massing. And we're about to make many of the same mistakes that were made in the city's first disastrous defense.
>
> The second battle of Atlanta doesn't pit an invading army against the home troops. It pits neighbor against neighbor. It's the battle of the city versus the suburbs, and like the Civil War, it's a battle nobody really wins.

The big idea of the speech was the second battle of Atlanta. The comparison between the first, military, battle and the second, political and economic, battle was valid and consistent throughout the speech.

13. *Humor:* As I said above, use humor only if it is original, you handle it well, and it is relevant to your subject.

THE BODY OF THE SPEECH

Organize the body of your speech in a logical pattern, keeping in mind the guidelines above, about subordinating little ideas to big ideas, and using personalized illustrations and simple, direct, visual language. Some specific suggestions about how to organize the body of your speech:

1. *Chronological order—the way it happened:* This structure is better suited to an informative speech than a persuasive one. It can be effective because it is straightforward and easily remembered. But don't use dates indiscriminately because people will not remember a long string of specific dates. Instead, structure it according to time periods and relate each time period to events. In a speech tracing a company's advertising methods from 1900 to the present, the speaker could talk about advertising at the turn of the century, leading up to the First World War, in the prosperous twenties, during the Depression, during and after World War II, in the complacent, home-centered fifties, during the political turmoil of the sixties, the boom years of the early seventies, the mid-seventies recession, and now.

2. *Inductive reasoning:* Inductive reasoning, or the scientific method of presenting evidence leading to a logical conclusion, is best suited for a persuasive speech. If you're arguing that no-fault insurance should be instituted in your state, you could describe how it has succeeded in other states and contrast this with events in your state, where no-fault insurance is not in effect.

3. *Deductive reasoning:* A deductive argument begins with a generalization, then draws a specific conclusion. For

example: "All men are born sinners and need to be saved: therefore you must repent and be saved." Or, "Every other teenager on the block has a car; therefore I should have one, too." Accepting this type of reasoning depends on accepting the validity of the premise (whereas inductive reasoning, in contrast, presents evidence to support a conclusion). So deductive reasoning is more useful in an emotional appeal than in a logical argument.

4. *Spelling out an acronym:* For example, E.A.S.Y., P.E.T. (Parent Effectiveness Training), T.A. (Transactional Analysis). This is best suited for an informative talk, since it makes key ideas easy for listeners to remember. However, it can lead to a persuasive appeal such as why you should learn to speak effectively, why you should take Parent Effectiveness Training, etc.

5. *Analogy:* "Mass transportation has worked in Toronto and it can work here too." "Learning to give a speech is like learning to play tennis." "The Battle of Atlanta in 1865 is similar to a political and economic battle being fought right now." Analogy is effective in the same way an anecdote or illustration is effective: It paints a vivid word picture that helps the audience remember the speaker's argument.

6. *Problem, cause, solution:* "A growing incidence of inner-city high school dropouts" [problem]; "an excessively academic curriculum that students find irrelevant to their everyday lives" [cause]; "inner-city storefront schools that attract kids off the street" [solution].

7. *Listing or enumerating:* "This company has three major concerns . . ." This is effective if the speaker limits the list. List five, maximum. Three is better.

8. *Chain thinking, or related ideas:* Examples: How the recession affected the U.S. politically, economically and socially. The physical, mental, emotional and spiritual health of this school's student body. Our company's past, its present and its future.

ENDING

Everything I said about the opening of your speech applies to the ending. Never let a speech peter out: It should end with a bang, not a whimper. Your ending should be as carefully planned and effective as your opening, because it is just as important to rivet the audience's attention when you make your final point as it is when you make your first. Also, knowing you have a strong, well-rehearsed ending prepared will help propel you throughout the speech. And if your speech is cut short for whatever reason, it helps to be able to wrap up quickly and incisively.

Any of the suggestions for opening can be used for the ending as well. Other suggestions:

1. *A repeat of the introduction or the method of the introduction:* A person speaking on fear of failure and how it interferes with success began a speech with "How much are you willing to risk?" After his talk he paused, looked at the audience, and repeated, "How much are *you* willing to risk?"

2. *Summary of main points of the speech:* A brief summary can help the audience remember the main points of the speech. However, if you use this method, beware of being turgid or academic. Make the summary brief, bright, staccato.

3. *Inducement:* This is effective in a persuasive speech. For example: "Won't you give so that the seven in this room who will be struck with cancer will have a chance?"

4. *Prophecy:* In a persuasive speech about the need to conserve gasoline: "If we continue to use gasoline at our present rate, we will have depleted all the world's known reserves within our lifetime." In an informative talk about the use of computers since the Second World War: "By the year

2000 computers will be as familiar to every American as the telephone is today."

5. *Group action:* For example, in a speech about public schools, a speaker could urge members of the audience to sign a sheet, committing themselves to working with the principal and teachers to effect some changes.

6. *Appeal to the emotions:* In an antiabortion speech: "Think of the youngest child in your family. Think of your youngest brother or sister. Maybe an economist would have advised you or your parents against taking on that extra financial burden. But imagine your family without that person, imagine all the nonmaterial riches you would have been deprived of. Human life is too precious for abortion to be condoned—ever."

RESEARCH

As a rule of thumb, don't accept an invitation to speak if you can't immediately rough out a general idea of what you want to say or if you think you will spend more than half your preparation time researching the subject. (An obvious exception, of course, would be a job-required presentation.)

I'm not saying you shouldn't do any research. Much of the excitement of speaking comes from its immediacy—audiences expect a speaker to have the latest information on the subject. So even if you know your subject inside out, you must be sure your information and facts are precise and up-to-date. I recommend doing as much reading around your subject—as well as reading material specifically related—as you have time for. Confidence comes from a thorough knowledge of your subject; if your fifteen-minute talk exhausts everything you know about it, you will dread the question-and-answer session.

CUTTING OR EXPANDING

A thorough knowledge of your subject also will give you flexibility, if you find you have more or less time to fill than you expected. In my experience, people usually have no trouble talking longer than they planned. They find it much more difficult to condense their remarks. It is much easier to go into a lot of detail than it is to express the essence of a subject.

When you find you have more time to fill than you anticipated, be careful of ad-libbing in an unfocused, rambling manner. If you have prepared a tightly organized, to-the-point ten-minute talk, you may dilute your message or lose your audience by tacking on an unrehearsed appendix. A better, more open-ended way to deal with the situation is to extend the question-and-answer session. Or, if you have to cut out material when you are preparing your speech, you might hold this in reserve. Or you can prepare answers to two or three questions you often are asked and use these if you find you have extra time to fill. I don't recommend preparing an extra, longer speech, just in case. Preparing one speech is enough work.

If you feel your subject doesn't merit any more time than you originally prepared for, or if you aren't familiar enough with a subject to fill more than a certain number of minutes, tell the chairperson so, or tell the audience. That's your prerogative.

Cutting a speech can be much more difficult. If you've prepared a twenty-minute speech and your turn to speak comes ten minutes before the group must break for lunch, you can handle it by saying, "I've prepared a twenty-minute talk and I don't feel ten minutes will do the subject justice, so I'll just answer a question I'm frequently asked," or, "I'll devote the few minutes we have to your questions"—and when questions are not immediately forthcoming, suggest some. When possible, of course, you should give a brief synopsis of the speech you prepared. If your speech is well organized and you've talked it through plenty of times, you should be able to get out your key ideas quickly.

Maintain an attitude of flexibility toward your speech. Don't regard it as a set piece that can't be tampered with. If you don't write it out word for word, it will be a little different every time you talk it through and you will be less likely to be thrown when you find that the time you have is not exactly what you expected.

Delivering Your Speech

FORGET THE RULES

Short of being rude, forget speech etiquette. For example, a lectern is a tool, not a barrier between you and your audience. Make it a point of orientation; it is there for you to use, not to control you. Sometimes you do have to stay behind a lectern for physical reasons. If the microphone is attached to it and you must use the mike to be heard, or if you're speaking at a luncheon and the lectern is set up behind a long head table, you probably won't have much choice. But whenever possible, request a neck microphone so that you won't get trapped behind a lectern.

A lectern is a useful place to set up your notes, your watch, your glass of water and anything else you may need during your speech. It also can be used as a tool to help you master the use of pauses. For example, if you're delivering a twenty-minute talk, you might deliver your opening from behind the lectern, then walk away from it to be closer to the audience as you launch into the body of your speech. When you finish making a point, when a pause feels right, if you're not sure what you want to say next, or if you feel a physical need to pause and breathe and get back with yourself for a moment, you can turn around and walk deliberately back to the lectern. Look down at your notes, check the time, take a drink of water or whatever you need to do, making no attempt to hide what you are doing from the audience. Then look up and make your next point, either from behind the lectern or after walking out in front of it, whichever feels comfortable and seems appropriate to the occasion.

Forget any rules you have been taught—about never putting your hands in your pockets, proper ways to stand, how to gesture to emphasize a point, how to gesture to indicate enthusiasm. It doesn't matter if you stand on your head while giving your speech, if that's the most effective way to get your point across. The point is to use whatever means necessary to achieve your end—making contact with your audience. The guidelines about body movement, centering and settling that I gave in Chapter 5 are valid only insofar as they help you get your message across to your audience.

DARE TO BE DIFFERENT

The same principle applies to the format of your speech. Don't be afraid to be different. If you've been allotted thirty minutes on a program, that doesn't mean you have to prepare a thirty-minute speech. If I'm asked to fill thirty minutes, I normally plan a fifteen- or twenty-minute speech and leave ten or fifteen minutes for questions and answers. But that is by no means a hard and fast rule. Start with a question-and-answer session, or spend the entire time on questions and answers if it seems appropriate. Toss out a few pertinent facts and leave the bulk of the time open for discussion. Carry on a dialogue with the coordinator of the meeting. Break people into small work groups and have the leader of each group report to the large group.

Ask the questions listed on pp. 148–50 and weigh the answers. Then decide what format will best serve your interests and those of your audience.

GETTING STARTED

Dispense with niceties unless they serve a definite purpose. Audiences are conditioned to being bored by speakers. The moment they hear the familiar "Thank you, Mr. Chairman. I am truly honored to have been invited to participate in this stimulating meeting," many tune out. That kind of remark usually is patently insincere, because most of the time the speaker is there because he wants to be and is going to get something out of it—a fee or an opportunity to promote his service, product or reputation. You don't have to recite *thank you*'s and ingratiating remarks to be polite. If you are genuinely grateful for a flattering introduction, say so personally to the person who introduced you, after you have finished speaking. That way he'll know you mean it.

Some speech teachers recommend starting a speech with a "dead phrase." The logic is that when you begin to speak, people will be shuffling, scraping their chairs, and getting settled, and may not hear your first few words. I strongly disagree. Stand up and remain silent until the room is absolutely quiet. Let the audience wait expectantly for a moment for you to begin. That way you are in control even before you open your mouth. Then start with a strong statement.

WATCH THE TIME

Unless your speech is being broadcast on radio or television, it probably doesn't matter if you speak seven minutes instead of five, or twenty-five minutes instead of twenty. But respect the value of your audience's time. When you are first asked to speak, find out how precisely timed the meeting will be. If the group has bi-weekly luncheon meetings, there may be a strict rule that they break at 2 P.M. If you are sandwiched between other speakers or seminars at a convention, you will upset the schedule if you exceed your time limit. Find out the time restrictions in advance, then watch the time as you talk. That's part of dealing with the reality. Putting your watch on the lectern can help.

On the other hand, if your time is up but you sense the audience would like to continue, ask them. Stop and say something like: "It seems to me there is still a lot of interest. I'm willing to continue, if you like. Is there a reason I must stop?"

VARY YOUR PACE

Keep the audience's interest alive by varying your pace, especially in a long speech. For example, if you're dealing with a depressing subject and you deliver a sombre thirty-minute speech without once lightening the tone, your audience may tune out.

You can vary your pace by asking a question, starting a dialogue with the audience, or simply by pausing, walking back to the lectern, and looking at your notes or taking a drink of water. A break gives the audience a breather, a chance to relax and absorb the material already presented before going on. And it makes you a human being.

VISUAL AIDS

I already have emphasized many times that when you speak, attention should be focused on you. If you keep this in mind, you will put visual aids in a proper perspective.

Visual aids should be used only when they reinforce or clarify an idea. They should never be used for the sake of novelty. Speakers commonly use visual aids as crutches or distractions. If a visual aid makes your ideas easier to understand or remember, use it; if not, don't.

Flip charts: Entire three-day seminars have been given on how to use a flip chart. I say let common sense and practice be your teacher. Obviously, the writing or diagram must be large enough for a person at the back of the room to see. If you're concerned with reaching out to your audience, you'll stand at the side of a flip chart instead of turning your back on your audience while you use it. If you practice using a flip chart before delivering your speech, you will realize that if you're right-handed, standing on the right-hand side of a flip chart makes it awkward to write or point something out on it.

Have a blank piece of paper covering the flip chart so that it won't distract the audience before you refer to it. Turn the page at the moment you are going to use it, and turn to a blank page when you are finished.

A flip chart can substitute for notes. For example, if you have three main points to emphasize, you can write each on a separate page of a flip chart. But that is a side benefit, not a reason to use the chart. Remember: Use a visual aid only if it helps the *audience* remember an idea or clarifies a point for them.

Slides: Audiovisual experts often recommend slides because they're polished and sophisticated. As you well know by now, I don't consider polish and sophistication the most important goals for a speaker. So use slides only if you are sure they get your point across better than you can verbally.

Experts often insist that the room be completely dark so the slides will show up best. The problem with that, of course, is that the slides become the thing, not the speaker. The audience won't even be able to see him. If you use slides, dim the lights, but don't turn them out completely. The slides may not look quite so beautiful, but you will maintain personal contact with your audience.

If you use a visual aid, maintain personal control of it, if at all possible. For example, if you're showing slides, press the switch that changes the slides yourself; if you're using a flip chart, flip the pages yourself. That way you remain in control of the sequence and the timing.

Finally, if you plan to use a visual aid, be prepared to go without it. The person responsible for setting up your flip chart might not do it; you might forget your marker; the extension cord might not be long enough. Any number of mechanical or electrical foul-ups might occur. Don't make your talk absolutely dependent on the aid; think out and practice an alternative.

THE MICROPHONE

A microphone will give you volume but it won't give you energy. Loudness is not equivalent to intensity; the microphone will give you the volume to reach out, but it will not put conviction into your voice.

It's hard to relax if you're using a fixed microphone, because you won't be able to move freely and you'll have to remain at the same distance from the microphone to keep your sound level constant. For this reason I suggest using a neck microphone whenever possible. Practice for using a neck mike by wearing a long cord with one end around your neck, and the other end tied to something, so that you learn to move freely without tripping over the cord.

Usually someone will be responsible for adjusting the microphone to a suitable volume, but if you suspect it is too loud or not loud enough, ask the audience. This is part of dealing with the reality.

The Manuscript Speech: To Read or Not to Read?

The manuscript speech is the biggest barrier to audience contact a speaker can have. Unless it is delivered exceptionally well, a manuscript speech seriously damages a speaker's credibility, prevents his personality from coming through, and destroys his natural rhythms of speech. How can a speaker expect to persuade an audience or make them believe he knows what he is talking about if he has to read everything he says? No matter how much expression a speaker uses, if he *reads* "I believe that the death penalty should be abolished," his words will not have nearly the impact they would have if he looked the audience in the eye and said the words straight.

The credibility of a person who reads a speech rarely approaches the credibility of a person who talks it. Even when a manuscript speech is written in conversational style and is read with a lot of energy and expression, it is not nearly as communicative as an extemporaneous speech unless the person reading it knows how to impose the hesitations, repetitions and pauses natural to spontaneous everyday speech. The average speaker's delivery of a manuscript speech is far too pat and perfect.

People who come to me wanting to deliver a manuscript speech often tell me they don't have time to memorize it and deliver it extemporaneously. My answer is, first, you shouldn't try to memorize the text; you should thoroughly familiarize yourself with the ideas in the manuscript speech. Usually this does not require an unreasonable amount of time or effort because most people speak on subjects they have considerable expertise in. Second, delivering a speech extemporaneously does not mean standing up in front of an audience without a single note. I never advise people to speak entirely without notes. (I use notes, although my "notes" often consist of no more than four or five words on a cue card.) I don't object to notes: They serve the dual purpose of prodding your memory and alleviating nervousness. What I *do* object to is reading words and sentences rather than expressing ideas. Manuscript speeches foster and encourage the former.

"Well," you may be thinking, "that's fine for experienced speakers, but I'm a novice. It's safer—and easier—for someone like me to stick with a manuscript." Wrong again. The irony is that it is the experienced speaker who delivers a manuscript speech well, not the novice. To deliver a manuscript speech well, you must be in control of your spoken image. You must be a good sight-reader. And you must be able to make reading sound like talking—no small task. You must know how to let yourself hesitate and stumble a bit, even let a few *um*'s and *uh*'s creep in so that it seems spontaneous and natural. You must break up the manuscript by ad-libbing in places. In short, you must be a seasoned performer. If you're not, you're better off speaking extemporaneously, with notes to prompt you if you need them.

I spend a lot of time working with people who bring in a manuscript speech, saying they must deliver it as is. Often, after talking it through several times, they realize they can get away from the manuscript by identifying the major ideas and putting them on cue cards. It usually takes no more time to reduce a manuscript speech to cue cards and deliver it extemporaneously than it does to work on delivering a manuscript speech until it comes alive and really expresses you.

ARE THERE ANY EXCEPTIONS?

"OK," you may be thinking, "I understand what you're saying but it's a little too idealistic. What if the information is very precise? What if a lot of figures are involved? What about a standard speech or policy supplied by the head office of an organization? What about the busy executive who doesn't have time to prepare his own speeches and must rely on his public relations department? What about the busy executive who doesn't have time to work with every single speech until he can deliver it extemporaneously? What about a speech that must follow slides word for word?"

First, the speech that must be concise or comprehensive or involves a lot of figures: As I have already emphasized in this chapter, people cannot absorb a lot of detailed information by ear. You're wasting your time and theirs if you read a detailed hour-long analysis of your company's financial situation. It would be much more effective to present the highlights and interpret the figures to explain what they say about the relative health of the organization, the direction it is going, and its financial outlook for the future. Then you can hand out the detailed analysis in written form for the audience to study at leisure. Also, when a lot of numbers are involved, visual aids can be helpful, because people find it much easier to remember figures when they see them. The visual aids can serve as your script.

Second, when your speech is handed down from the head office: If you are representing your organization on a policy matter, part of your job is to thoroughly understand its details, ramifications and implications. Your organization's credibility comes from you, not the printed statement, so you should discuss the policy in your own words. Remember, to your audience, *you* are the organization you represent. So if you read your company's policy as if it had nothing to do with you personally, you are undermining your company's image and credibility. If legalities are involved, you can read certain sections, prefacing them with something like: "I will have to read this part to you to be sure the company's position on this particular matter is absolutely clear."

All this said, I realize that delivering a manuscript speech is unavoidable at times, particularly for busy executives. It may also be necessary for sophisticated audiovisual presentations when cues are very important. If, for whatever reason, you must deliver a manuscript speech, note the following:

Delivering the Manuscript

IMPOSE YOUR PERSONALITY

No matter how infallible the authority who has given you a speech to deliver, don't be afraid to change the format or the exact wording. No wording is so valuable or profound that it cannot be changed to one you are more comfortable with or which better expresses your personality.

For some reason, people tend to regard words on a printed page as untouchable. They pick up a manuscript speech and their immediate goal is to read it exactly as it was written. They practice to make their delivery perfect, instead of practicing to make it real and alive. They become concerned that clever phrases come out just right. It's not important that a speaker deliver clever gems and turns of phrase; it's important that what comes out of his mouth is direct and authentic.

The only way to make a manuscript speech workable is to read it aloud with a pen in hand, ready to change words and word constructions until it says what you want to say, the way you would say it, not the way the speechwriter wrote it. When I work with a person on a manuscript speech, we play with the wording, change and adapt it until the speaker is comfortable with it, has imposed his personality on it, and can get away from it in a couple of places.

Here's how one speaker changed his manuscript introduction to suit his personal style (please note: / = pause):

Thank**S** ~~you very much,~~ Barbara. ~~I know that this meeting will be one of the most rewarding and fun-filled get-togethers this department has ever~~

~~had. As you've just seen, in the introduction of~~
~~Walter Jones, it's already gotten off to a rousing~~
~~start.~~ But if the sketch ~~you just heard~~ were about 1987
and your accomplishments during
~~that~~ *1987* ~~year~~ instead of "What's my job?" it
should have been entitled "What a job!" because
that, ladies and gentlemen ⁄sums up
the kind of year it was.

When he finished editing, it looked like this:

> Thanks, Barbara / Ladies and gentlemen / the sketch you
> just heard was about your accomplishments during 1987. /
> But, instead of "What's my job?" / it should have been
> "What a job!" / because that sums up the kind of year it
> was. /

This was much closer to his own direct style of speaking.

THE OPENING: COMING ACROSS AS A PERSON

The opening of any speech is important, but the opening of a
manuscript speech is crucial. Even if you are going to read
ninety percent of your speech, you should take the time to
practice delivering an extemporaneous opening if you want the
audience to listen at all. Audiences are numbed to boring
manuscript speeches and often the only reason they even attempt to listen is out of respect for the speaker's credentials.
One of the major problems of manuscript speeches is that they
prevent the flavor of the speaker's personality from coming
through. So be sure the opening to a manuscript speech not
only makes the audience sit up and listen but lets you come
across as a person as well. For example, a speaker presenting a
rather dry financial report began: "Research can be the art of

gathering facts and drawing your own confusion." Then he cited some humorous, meaningless statistics such as: "Eighty percent of people who commit suicide are coffee, tea or beer drinkers." The humor was relevant to his talk, he caught the audience's interest, and he came across as a person as well.

HOW TO READ IT

The manuscript speech should, as much as possible, sound as if you are talking it. It should be marked with vertical lines for pauses, because often the reader forgets that pausing is a part of normal conversation. When you practice, use a recorder. Does it sound like someone talking to a group, or does it sound like someone reading?

Practice to have as much direct eye contact as possible, especially on openings, closings, and personal comments such as "I think this is important." Remember, the aim is to be as natural and conversational as you can.

IF SOMEONE ELSE HELPS PREPARE YOUR SPEECH

Although ideally I think people should prepare their own speeches, so that they will best express their own personalities and ideas, I understand how time-consuming researching and organizing a speech can be. I realize many busy executives often have to let someone else do this for them.

If someone else is preparing your speech, it is important to remember two things: Take the time to fully discuss with him what you want to say, and take the time to work with the product he delivers until you make it your own.

Many executives slough off responsibility for their own speeches by throwing a general topic at their public relations department and saying, "Say what you think needs to be said." They usually get what they deserve—a speech that may or may not be well-written, depending on the competence of the speechwriter, but which probably will not reflect them as a person and may not even accurately reflect the organization. On the other hand, the speechwriter sometimes attempts to take over and tell the executive what he needs to say. In this case, the burden is on the speaker to be sure that the speechwriter knows the main points he wants covered and understands his individual style. So it's a give and take situation.

If another person is helping you prepare your speech, your minimum input should be deciding on your approach and the main points you want to make. Then you can meet with the speechwriter, explain the direction you want the speech to take, and give him a chance to ask questions. Give the speechwriter as much access to your time as possible, to exchange ideas. If you can, develop a working relationship with one speechwriter so that he can develop an understanding of your specialty and a feel for your speaking style.

If you're busy, other people can help you in ways other than writing manuscript speeches for you. You can say to an assistant, "OK, I'm giving a speech to so-and-so and I want to cover these main points. I need a good example of a school involved in this kind of program." Or, "I need you to find out for me what has been written about the pros and cons of air bags and safety belts." Or, "Get me the latest statistics on the hiring of minority groups in the federal government." You can prepare the basic outline of a speech and ask your assistant to think of a lively introduction or colorful anecdotes to illustrate your main points. Or, once you've decided on an approach, you can have your assistant prepare an outline and you can flesh it out.

10

Special Speaking
Situations

Interviews

The prospect of being interviewed by the press terrifies many
people. They tend to assume that the press is a natural enemy,
that it is out to "get" them. Sometimes this *is* the case; when it
is, it should be handled like any other hostile speaking situation, using the active listening techniques outlined in Chapters
7 and 8. But in most cases the press, like any other audience,
simply wants to hear an interesting "story"—whether that
story is informative, entertaining or controversial. The press is
really just an intermediary between you, the speaker, and your
end audience, the public: It funnels information from one to
the other. If you practice the same communications skills that
you would in any other speaking situation, you probably will
get your message across to the public. I say "probably" because
the competence, ethical standards and objectivity of the re-

porter do affect the way you will communicate with your audience. But it's mostly up to you.

Prepare for a press interview the same way you would for any question-and-answer session (see Chapter 8). Anticipate questions you might receive and practice answering them aloud, either to a colleague or into your tape recorder. You can also try to beat the press at its own game: Since some reporters don't have time to do a lot of research about you or your subject before interviewing you, you may be able to influence the kinds of questions they ask by providing them with written information before the interview.

Let's look at interviews in the three media—television, radio and print.

THE TELEVISION INTERVIEW

A television interview tends to scare people more than any other kind of media interview because they feel they have much more to deal with. There are the behind-the-scenes, electronic mysteries of television to contend with, as well as the television audience—all the more frightening because it is invisible.

We fear most the things we don't understand, so familiarizing yourself with the inside of a television studio will diminish your fears considerably. If you are scheduled for an interview, you probably will be able to arrange a guided tour; if not, call the television stations in your community and find out if any programs welcome live audiences. Second, don't let the television audience concern you. Your immediate audience is the person interviewing you; you should focus your attention on him. Think of the television audience as an eavesdropper on a conversation you are having with one other person.

Two or three cameras will be set up; the one with the red light on is the one currently in use. Never play to the camera unless you are giving an address or telephone number or some other message specifically aimed at the viewing audience rather than the interviewer. The television audience is watching a conversation between two people; there is nothing more absurd than seeing two people talking who don't look at each other.

A television studio is a buzz of activity: Technicians stroll around the studio behind the camera, people give obscure hand signals, stagehands rearrange the set, visitors walk through. Don't allow yourself to become distracted. Practice the relaxation techniques outlined in Chapter 5: Breathe, get with yourself, then deal with the here and now, which is the dialogue between you and the interviewer.

Don't attempt to understand or control the technical details of the interview. Unlike other speaking situations, during an interview it is not your responsibility to be in control of anything except yourself. The technical aspects of the program are the host's responsibility. If the lighting is wrong, the camera angles inept, the timing bad, there is nothing you can do about it—and it will reflect on the television station, not you. The same applies to nontechnical details: If there is a silence, it's not up to you to fill it (unless you've just been asked a question); if a stagehand drops something, it's up to the host to deal with it. One exception would be a hand signal explained to you before the interview begins. For example, the host might tell you he will signal in a certain way if time is short and you have to wrap up your answer quickly.

A television interview is more intimate visually and aurally than a speech to a live audience. The television audience will be able to see you as close up as someone who kisses you; and you will not have to project your voice any more than you would in a normal one-to-one conversation. Movement is magnified on television, so in a seated interview don't use exaggerated body movements.

Ask about makeup and appropriate clothing. For women, a

little more makeup than you usually wear is best, because the bright lights fade your complexion. I recommend that men leave makeup to the studio's discretion (however, they should make sure shiny foreheads are powdered). Solid colors or stripes are better than busy patterns. Keep hair simple and wear a minimum of jewelry or anything else that might make noise, catch the lights or draw attention to itself.

THE RADIO INTERVIEW

The technical paraphernalia at radio stations is not nearly so intimidating as that of television studios. Your interview will be broadcast in a small soundproof room with no distractions. Go through the relaxation techniques described in Chapter 5. Then concentrate on the interviewer.

Radio, like television, does not require the kind of voice projection you need when you give a speech. An engineer will ask you for a sound level on your voice and set the microphone at the proper volume. When being tested, be sure to speak in a normal tone of voice so that the microphone will be set right during the interview. Don't worry about the sound of your voice or the way you articulate any more than you would for any other speech (see Chapter 6). It's the engineer's job to ensure that your voice comes across clearly to the radio listeners.

People sometimes say that a radio interview worries them less than a television interview because they don't have to worry about how they look. Personally, I much prefer television because I feel total communication is important and radio cuts off the nonverbal aspect. I've seen radio commentators doing all sorts of phony things with their voices while their bodies showed they were not being authentic. Television doesn't allow this. Body language helps us communicate our message; when it is taken away, we are robbed of one important dimension of communication.

On radio, the sound of your voice and the words you choose must communicate your message. Remember that all your energy must be expressed through your voice: You can't rely on your face or your body to help. So be especially concerned about the energy level in your voice, keeping in mind that speaking with energy means speaking with feeling and saying everything as if you mean it—not speaking loudly.

THE WRITTEN INTERVIEW

An interview with a print reporter usually is much more relaxed than a radio or television interview because there is no strict time limit. You can ponder questions, you can say, "Give me a moment to think about that one," and you can hold a silence.

Consider the reporter your audience. Everything I have said about establishing rapport with an audience—reaching out, bending and adapting—applies to your relationship with a reporter.

However, if you establish rapport and the interview begins to resemble a relaxed one-to-one conversation, don't make the mistake of completely letting down and treating the reporter as a friend or confidante. Keep reminding yourself that everything you say can be quoted. Most reporters respect "off the record" remarks, but it is still safer to say you cannot comment on a subject—and a "no comment" doesn't come across nearly as strong in print as it does on radio or television.

A written interview is more one-dimensional than a radio interview, because you cannot even rely on the tone of your voice to clarify your meaning; all there is are your words in cold print. However, in many articles—feature articles particularly—the writer describes your tone of voice, your appearance, your personality, his overall impressions of you.

You cannot control the competence or the accuracy of his writing, so forget about that and try to influence the tone of what he writes by concentrating on the same things you would in any speaking situation: developing rapport with the reporter/audience, and being direct and authentic.

Using the Telephone

In most interview situations, you have the advantage of personal contact with the interviewer. On the telephone you have no personal contact at all; all you have is the sound of your voice and the words you use.

We use the telphone so much that we take for granted its effectiveness as a tool of communication. The better we know the person we are talking with, the more we tend to assume he understands what we mean. Yet—and I cannot emphasize this strongly enough—you can never be sure you have been understood until you ask a question and listen to the response. For this reason, it is important not to talk for an extended period of time without pausing and getting a response from the person you are talking to.

Because the telephone is an impersonal medium, it is easier to argue or say no than it is when you have to deal with a person face to face. How often have you found it easy to refuse to contribute time or money over the telephone but next to impossible when you are asked to do so personally? On the other hand, you cannot hold a silence for long over the telephone; so if you want to argue, prepare your ideas well because you'll have to rely on verbal dynamics alone.

The telephone is one of our most important and most frequently used tools of communication in both our jobs and our personal lives, so it is important not to take for granted the way we communicate by telephone. Check your spoken image over the telephone by leaving a tape recorder next to it. Tape your end of conversations for a week or two, to give yourself time to forget about the tape recorder and be natural. Then, when you have a quiet time, listen to it all at once. Check for the basic vocal qualities already discussed. Imagine you are on the other end, listening: What kind of image are you sending out?

Business Presentations

When businesspeople make presentations about their product or company they often get caught up in the details of their subject and forget the cardinal difference between written and spoken communication—the physical presence of the speaker. I said it in Chapter 3 and I will say it again: The audience may forget every word you say, but they will retain a flavor of you.

Every company promotes its product as unique or better than its competitors'. That's what free enterprise is all about. But whether or not you want to admit it, your product or your company probably isn't all that unique, and chances are someone else makes as good a mousetrap as yours. To sell your company or your product you must sell yourself.

I remember being invited to critique a presentation about an innovative software package. The company had prepared a glossy booklet about the software; the speaker passed copies around the audience, then proceeded to read it out loud. I helped him change this to a slide presentation, followed by a question-and-answer session. Then, just before the audience left, the speaker would pass out the booklets. The booklet neatly reinforced the slide presentation; it was more detailed but followed the same format. After seeing the slide presentation, members of the audience could leaf through the booklet and immediately relate to it. Adding the slide presentation and the question-and-answer period allowed the speaker to impose his personality on the presentation—and how he came across to the audience was just as important to the sale of his product as the professionalism of the slide presentation or the booklet.

When preparing a sales presentation, take time to research the prospective buyers' needs, the products they presently are using, their future plans. Then use the following approach: "We know you have three concerns. Our product can help you meet those concerns in these ways. . . ." Always keep in mind that you sell your product by selling yourself.

Board rooms are the scenes of some of the driest, dullest speeches in the business world. There simply is no excuse for reading a quarterly financial report. You may argue, "Well, if you hand it out, people won't read it." True, but if you read it, no one will listen, so you're no further ahead. Board room presentations should be tightly organized, extemporaneous talks lasting no more than five or ten minutes, followed by a question-and-answer period. If a lot of figures are being discussed, a flip chart can help.

Remember, business presentations should meet all the standards of an effective speech. Don't think of them as a different category.

11

Men and Women Together

Affirmative action and the women's movement have produced a rash of books and articles dealing with women's special problems in developing assertiveness and managerial skills and getting ahead in their careers.

Women also have special speaking problems just because they're women. But men have special speaking problems just because they're men, too. I strongly believe that men and women should not be trained separately in communications workshops, assertiveness development seminars, managerial training groups or whatever. The world is not segregated by sex; men and women work and live together and must learn to deal with one another. Women are not interested in learning how to become more effective managers or speakers so that they can manage or speak to other women. In most cases their working environment is dominated by men, so more than anything else, they want to develop managerial or communications skills that are effective with men. Seminars for women give women practice performing in front of other women only, and give them feedback from other women only. In most cases this doesn't solve their problems, because women usually fear speaking and being assertive most in front of men.

My seminars are open to men and women, and both sexes benefit from feedback from the other. There usually are more men than women, however, because most people who come to my seminars are in managerial positions, and management is still overhwhelmingly dominated by men. Occasionally, however, there are more women than men. The first time this happened—there were seven women and two men—I considered informing the men of the imbalance, in case they objected to participating in a predominately female group. When I suggested this to my administrator, she rejoined: "Why do you think you should tell the men they're outnumbered? You wouldn't do the same if it were the other way around." She was right, of course, and I was ashamed to have lapsed into a knee-jerk sexist reaction.

I was particularly sensitive to the interaction between the sexes in that seminar and it made me more acutely aware of the special ways men and women can learn from one another when they're together in a controlled, nonthreatening learning environment.

Both men and women come to my seminars either because they're uncomfortable speaking to a group or because they speak a lot and want to improve their performance so that they can become the best they can be. The men typically are concerned with how businesslike, authoritative and in control they are. Most fall into the computer category: They're very controlled and afraid to show their feelings because of their concern with being taken seriously when they speak. Often they have taken public speaking instruction sometime in the past and are preoccupied with rules about what they should and should not do.

Women are concerned about projecting authority, too, but typically they approach it from the opposite end of the spectrum. They usually are much less fearful about revealing their feelings and inner selves, but they're afraid that if they are the least bit direct or show any real strength they will lose their femininity and project an abrasive or aggressive image. Women tend to be apologizers. They use little-girl, flirtatious or manipulative ways to get their message across because they're afraid to risk expressing themselves in a strong way.

How Men and Women Learn from One Another

Women demonstrate to men how it is possible to let down their defenses a little and express feelings, how they can loosen up their bodies, move more easily, and gesture more naturally, without letting their emotions take over, losing control, or appearing ambivalent or vacillating. The men teach the women that it is possible to be assertive without becoming tough or aggressive, and that men do *not* respect or admire so-called "feminine" ways in a speaking situation. The interaction can make men and women both more sensitive to each other. A manager of a textile factory mainly staffed by women commented that listening to the concerns expressed by women in the seminar would make him a more understanding employer.

The Masculine Myth

AUTHORITY AND MASCULINITY

Men who concentrate on projecting authority often do so to mask insecurity. The inconsistency between the image they try to project and the real person they are inside creates a credibility gap. Stuart, a young businessman with political ambitions, was overly intent on being taken seriously because of his age. He had a full beard because he felt it added weight to his still-boyish face, and he always wore conservatively cut three-piece suits. He spoke with a lot of energy and downward inflection in his voice and he projected surface warmth toward his audience. But he was so concerned with being an authority figure that he condescended. He used unnecessarily complex language, and when his talk touched on a legal technicality, he would smile and say something patronizing like, "Now you won't know what probate means; it's the official validation of a person's will"—when it was entirely possible that some members of the audience would be familiar with the term.

Stuart's overall image was pompous and phony. The other students in the seminar commended him for his articulateness, intelligence, organization and bearing, but criticized him for being insensitive and condescending. His problem, of course, was that inside he was very unsure of himself and he wanted to hide his uncertainty from his audience. But as I've emphasized a hundred times already, if you try to project something that's inconsistent with your inner self, you will lose credibility. I'm not saying that Stuart should have projected insecurity. But he needed to get rid of his phony air of superiority and relate to the audience as his equal.

Sometimes men project more authority than they want to. When I was giving my opening talk at the beginning of a seminar, I wondered if I was getting across to one student in particular. He was a banker—a large, impeccably dressed man with a deadpan face. When he did show a flicker of expression, it was invariably negative. Later he mentioned he had a problem communicating with his employees because many of them seemed to be afraid of him. He couldn't understand why, he said, because inside he felt like a warm, reasonably understanding person. When he saw himself on videotape he began to understand that his lack of facial expression, combined with his size, careful grooming and conservative clothing, were all working to push people away.

Shortly after he had begun working at the bank, his superior told him he was too casual and familiar and would have to straighten up and be more serious if he wanted to be successful. Seventeen years later he was still heeding that message. It was typical of the "masculine" messages men receive all their lives: Pull your shoulders back. Don't be a sissy. Be a man. You've got to be on top of things. Don't let down your defenses for a minute because, if you do, you might lose control of the situation.

TOO IMPORTANT TO RELAX

Having received messages like that all their lives, men are much more apt to resist my relaxation techniques than are women. Some adopt the attitude: "I may go through the routine before I go to bed at night, but during the day at the office, I've got to be tense if I want to get anything done." They're afraid that if they relax they will lose control. Or they think, "If you're not under pressure, you're not important." One way of letting the world know you're important is by never letting down, never relaxing, and never letting yourself come across in a warm, caring way—because you have more important things on your mind. I recall one business executive who never relaxed, even when sitting quietly in a chair listening to someone speak. When I told him he would have to deal with the tension in his body if he wanted to become a more effective speaker, he listened. But as he was leaving the seminar on the last day, his last words were: "I'm still not convinced that tension is really a bad thing." He was unwilling to risk trying another way.

Being in control is important to the male mystique. It's much more difficult for men than for women to open up to an audience and establish intimacy, because intimacy can expose weaknesses. To help people relax and get to know one another at the beginning of my seminar, I often ask each person to give a short talk in answer to the question, "Who am I?" The men usually talk in great detail about their work background and present job, and to wrap up, throw in a few superficial remarks about their personal lives. The women go into greater depth about their personal lives and are much more likely to talk about their goals, ambitions and feelings about life in general. Women sometimes inject personal opinion or experience at the expense of objective data and analysis to back up their views. But men often are so concerned with appearing authoritative that they appear personally detached from the issue they are arguing and lose the impact that personal involvement adds.

Jem, a young attorney, was a super-jock. Most men "test the water" by wearing business suits to the seminar the first day, but Jem came the first day dressed in corduroy pants and a turtleneck sweater. He was a good-looking man with a powerful physique, and his body movements emphasized his energy and strength. He lived in an inner-city neighborhood and personally was very committed to revitalizing the inner city. But, equating feelings with weakness, he talked about broad issues instead of his own involvement. His argument would have been much more compelling if he had taken the risk of letting his own deep feelings show through.

THE MOTIVATIONAL HIGH-PRESSURE SALESMAN

Another way the male concern with control can be expressed is in a motivational high-pressure-salesman image. An efficiency expert in one of my seminars answered this description. The moment he began to speak, his energy filled the room like an electrical charge. He organized his ideas superbly and delivered them with the conviction and zeal of an evangelical preacher. His energy was so compelling that the audience sat up and listened with a vengeance—at first. But after a few minutes they would turn off in a kind of symbolic self-defense, because his energy was so overwhelming they felt attacked rather than talked to.

The driving urge of this kind of person to convince others of his ideas, control the audience, and set himself up as an infallible authority makes him lose touch with his own energy level. Sean, an FAA airplane crash investigator who had had to perform for years under a great deal of pressure, had developed a super-energetic, dogmatic speaking style that had proven effective for him in his job. No matter what he talked about in class, he would begin full-steam, never giving anyone else a chance to get a word in edgewise. His body betrayed the tension he was holding inside: He paced nervously and clenched his fists as he talked.

I felt that if he could get rid of the tension in his body, lower his energy level, and learn to be sensitive to his audience, he would be an excellent speaker. After we went through the breathing for relaxation exercise, I gave him an assignment for the next day to talk quietly to each person in the room, individually.

The next day he stood up to speak and said, "Yesterday I thought this assignment was a bit ridiculous. Today I feel different. Who would have thought I would have to stop smoking in order to learn to communicate? But now I don't have to blow smoke any more."

The breathing exercise had relaxed him so completely that he had given up smoking literally overnight. (A year later he was still not smoking.) But when he said he didn't have to blow smoke any more, he meant he didn't have to sound off any more. To his surprise, he found he could relax, be himself and come across with half the energy, and still be effective.

The Feminine Myth

The women's movement has aggravated a basic conflict within many women: On the one hand, they want to be independent and self-sufficient; on the other, they want meaningful and rewarding relationships with men. To prove that they haven't sacrificed men on the altar of liberation, many women feel they must retain an ounce of "femininity" to balance every ounce of independence. This struggle between so-called femininity and independence is the source of the problem most women have with their spoken image. They feel intelligent, capable, independent and assertive inside, but externally they still project all the "feminine" qualities of softness, shyness, uncertainty, deference and sexiness.

I don't want to help women develop tough outer shells. I do want to help them bring their inner and outer selves together, help them express authentically and directly the strength they feel inside. When women are successful in bringing the two together, they realize that they can lose little-girl ways and express themselves as mature adults, without denying their sexuality or turning into tough, aggressive "broads."

Women often don't realize the disparity between what they feel and what they project. The first shock of recognition comes from seeing themselves on videotape. Invariably, they dislike what they see. But negative feedback from men in the seminar is by far the most effective way of convincing women that a stereotyped feminine image does not help them. Women use feminine ways because of cultural conditioning and because they think men expect it and like it. When men tell them straight that they don't, it's usually enough to motivate women to begin making changes. In a seminar composed of seven men and one woman, the men consistently commended the woman on qualities such as intelligence, good diction, good organization of her subject matter, sincerity, warmth and body move-ment. They consistently criticized her for her "feminine" stance—for girlishness, too soft a voice, too low an energy level, shyness, lack of self-assertiveness, and too much smiling. Comments like this from successful men in executive positions convince women that they can shed "feminine" ways without the risk of losing appeal to men—faster than dozens of aca-demic assurances or arguments from other women about the value of assertiveness.

A few examples should make this clearer.

ALICE IN WONDERLAND

Kelly, a twenty-four-year-old, very pretty junior bank officer, was fond of wearing pinafore dresses. The dresses, combined with sleek, long, blond hair, made her reminiscent of Alice in Wonderland. Her voice matched her appearance: It was soft, girlish and had a lot of upward inflection. Despite her appear-ance and voice, Kelly was an intelligent, ambitious young woman who took herself very seriously. When she saw herself on videotape, she saw and heard the Alice in Wonderland image. She cut her hair to shoulder length, began wearing more tailored clothing, taped her voice, and began working for a fuller tone and more downward inflection. But when she listened to her "new" voice on tape, she thought it sounded "flat and aggressive." The other students strongly disagreed with her. They pointed out to her that, on a continuum, her voice had been so far in the direction of sugary sweetness that she would have a long way to go before acquiring a voice that could be described as anything close to flat or aggressive. Kelly was so used to injecting a phony lilt into her voice that any change sounded extreme in comparison. Her experience illustrates, our spoken image is as ingrained as our habits of dressing and grooming. We cannot expect to make drastic changes overnight. We have to make them gradually, test them, and learn to live with them.

THE CHINA DOLL

Jerri was another version of the smiley, little-girl image many women project. But because Jerri was a stockbroker in her early forties, the little-girl affectation rang even more false than it did in Kelly's case.

Jerri's appearance made it obvious she was a perfectionist. Her clothes were fiercely coordinated—lime-green suit with green-and-white polka-dot blouse, green shoes, bracelet and earrings, and the like. There was never a hair out of place in her lacquered, close-to-the-face, ear-length pageboy. She had two perfect circles of rouge on each cheek, which in combination with her stiff hairdo, large eyes and round face made her look like a dewy-eyed, freshly painted china doll just off the shelf.

Jerri reinforced the dolly look when she spoke. One of her first talks was about a trip she had taken to the Mediterranean. She told the story with an air of wide-eyed wonderment, constantly smiling and tilting her head to one side in a placating posture.

It was Jerri's nature to be meticulous, and I didn't encourage her to change that. But over the years, she had carried her concern with perfection to an extreme—witness the hairdo and rouge. When I commented on her hair, she said she had been wearing it that way for ten years and had finally gotten it to the point where it was perfect. And the rouge? She thought it blended into her face. She had no idea it was so obtrusive.

Jerri is an example of a person totally out of touch with her image. She didn't realize how "grinny" she was, how silly the rouge on her cheeks looked. She really didn't know how she looked at all. When she saw herself on videotape and got some feedback from the other students in the class, she began to see herself as others saw her. Despite her meticulousness, she was not inflexible. She was willing to take risks and to change, as she put it, "a little at a time."

By the final evening of the seminar Jerri had changed more than a little. She spoke to the fifty people present for the group's "graduation" about her four years as a stockbroker—how it was generally considered a man's job, and about the trouble she had had being accepted. She told the story straight, without any of the silly grinning she formerly had used to punctuate every sentence, and ended with: "And here I am, four years later, just one of the boys."

SOFT AND SEXY

Sally, a pretty, well-proportioned, intelligent and ambitious young businesswoman, attended my seminar the first morning wearing a silky, crimson, figure-hugging dress. It was an attractive dress: It flattered her figure, and the color was becoming. The following day she wore a suit and I commented to her, "By the way, I think the outfit you are wearing today is much more appropriate." She got very defensive and said she spent a lot of time choosing her wardrobe and thought the red dress was very attractive.

Two of the men in the seminar interjected, "Oh, Sandy, I think you're being too particular. There was nothing wrong with that dress. I really think Sally looked great in it." Naturally, Sally beamed with the positive male reinforcement. But a third man, an attorney, looked at Sally very straight and said, "Sally, I'm telling you that I think that the image you project in that dress is not the image you want to project in a business situation." Sally remained unconvinced. Then a man who had remained silent until then said brightly, "Hey, Sally, *I* really LIKE you in that dress."

Sally heard what he was saying. She saves that dress for cocktail parties now.

My point is this: Part of being prepared and in control of a speaking situation is being aware of the visual image you project and being prepared to take the consequences of that image. A woman whose dress projects a sexy image had better be prepared to take the consequences. Her audience, especially if it is predominately male, may receive her warmly, but they won't take her as seriously as they would if she were dressed less suggestively.

If you are a woman and being taken seriously when you speak is important to you, take a careful look at your visual image. Jangly bracelets, dangling earrings and the like send out an image of frivolousness. Long hair tends to project an unprofessional, little-girl or sexual image. Excessively form-fitting or revealing clothes call attention to your body and distract from your message.

I'm not advising you to deny your sexuality or give up femininity. It's a question of appropriateness. If you're a rock musician or a movie star, outrageous or sexy clothing may be part of the image you want to project. But if you're not, a speaking situation is not an appropriate place for a woman—or a man, for that matter—to project a "sexy" image, if she wants to be taken seriously. As a rule of thumb, choose clothing that doesn't distract from your message. Sexy clothes distract. Flashy jewelry distracts. Sloppiness of any kind distracts.

The male suit-and-tie business uniform allows men a professional look with no overtones of sexuality. It's tailored but it's not form-fitting. A woman who wears a tight sweater and a short skirt to speak is equivalent to a man wearing a skinny T-shirt and tight jeans.

As a businesswoman, I usually wear a jacket when I speak. Dresses or blouses and skirts can be attractive, but a jacket gives a crisper, more professional, more finished look. A businessman wouldn't speak in shirtsleeves, so why should I, as a woman, adopt less professional standards for myself?

I do *not*, however, adopt a pseudo-male uniform. I like to wear soft blouses under my jacket, complemented by a scarf or silk flower.

How I dress is one way of telling my audience who I am. I never mirror my audience in my dress. For example, if I am invited to speak to a woman's garden club and I know they will be wearing skirts, pants and sweaters, I still speak to them wearing my business attire. I can adapt and reach out to my audience in other ways.

Being in full control of your visual image is one step toward gaining control of your spoken image.

LITTLE-GIRL POSE

It's a long way from the placating, little-girl ways women so often adopt to the style of what people would call a tough, aggressive "broad." But when women try to reconcile the strength they feel with the image they project, they sometimes go too far with it. The visual image of Carla, a thirty-five-year-old advertising copywriter living in New York, labeled her as a strong, possibly aggressive, woman. She dressed in the height of fashion, bordering on the avant-garde; her hair was frizzed, and she wore tinted glasses. She looked as if she probably would speak like Germaine Greer. But when she opened her mouth, a little-girl voice and simpering smile came out.

The other students told her they didn't believe the little-girl pose, so when the group practiced role-playing I suggested to Carla that she act out an aggressive role. She played the part of a person who had been left a lot of stock, speaking to a board of directors. She really came on strong—heartless, single-minded, ruthless. The class told her that while the role she had played was too sharp and abrasive, it was more believable than the little-girl act. Carla pointed to a real-estate agent in the class, also a woman, and said, "Why will you take a strong stance from Judy and not from me? [Judy had no trouble being straight with her audience.] I have the same problem all the time. Whenever I let down and let people see my real self, they react negatively." One of the men in the class responded, "It seems to me that as long as you show your audience that you care about them, you can be what some people would term a 'tough broad.' "

Like Carla, many women think there are only two choices: sweet little girl or tough, aggressive broad. If a woman says, "OK, I'm not going to let this audience push me around. I believe X, Y, and Z on this subject and I'm going to let them know it," she blocks off her awareness and loses sensitivity to her audience. So of course she gets a negative reaction. Then she says, "See? People won't accept me when I'm assertive."

The Masculine, the Feminine and the Balanced Person

Books have been written on the distinction between assertiveness and aggressiveness. But a woman in one of my classes struck the nerve of the entire issue. Recently married, Elsa was struggling between career ambitions and her desire to have children and stay at home with them. Her basic conflict was between a desire to achieve with no holds barred and a desire to be "feminine." She gave a talk on her distorted, stereotyped interpretations of the terms "femininity" and "masculinity." Then she described a third image which she called asexual but which I prefer to call the balanced person, and I have substituted "balanced" for "asexual" in her speech.

"Femininity," Elsa said, "is being gentle, kind, attentive, personable, friendly, understanding and warm. There is a tendency in being feminine to skirt the issue a little and not really get to the point of a subject because it's acceptable for a feminine person to be a little indecisive. She can get by with a little naïveté on a subject and be a little coquettish. The feminine speaker gets her audience to look *at* her instead of *to* her for her message.

"Masculinity is commanding. Masculinity is being organized and able to speak with authority on a subject. A masculine speaker makes his audience pay attention to him and to what he is saying. He commands what he says because he is sure of what he is talking about. He doesn't have to worry about what his audience is thinking because he knows what *he* is thinking and that's the important thing.

"A balanced person doesn't have to depend on being authoritative or coquettish to get a point across or to win the audience over. The balanced person has a balance of emotions along with a balanced stance. He can let himself show happiness, sadness or anger without letting his emotions take control. The balanced person knows his subject matter and presents it in such a way that the audience sits up and listens. But he also is intuitive and cares about the audience's feelings and ideas. He is in control of the situation, but he doesn't force his message on his audience. He knows how to zero in to find out whether his audience is with him, but he doesn't embarrass anyone or put anyone on the spot. A balanced person is not afraid of questions about his subject matter or of arguments about his point of view, because he understands that there are different points of view about his subject and he is prepared to defend his own position and take the consequences. The balanced person is not afraid of being human. If he makes a mistake, he is straight about it, admits it, and then gets on with the business at hand."

Elsa had been the personification of the struggle between femininity and masculinity throughout the seminar. Her voice

and energy level were masculine: She spoke in a forceful, compelling voice, had plenty of energy, and used it to reach out to
the audience. But she also communicated her energy through
her body, and her body conveyed unadulterated femininity in
motion. She swiveled her hips, literally shimmied when she
moved, and smiled flirtatiously. During the course of the seminar Elsa became painfully aware of the contradictory image she
was sending out and how it related to the conflicts within her.
She delivered the talk on masculinity, femininity and balance
on the last day of the seminar. As she talked through her definitions, her body mirrored what she was saying. When she
talked about femininity, her voice was soft and she used
suggestive body movements. When she talked about masculinity, her voice became more forceful, she stood with her feet
planted firmly and well apart, her gestures were clipped, and
she dispensed with the suggestive body movement. When she
talked about balance, her body and voice lost all connotations
of sex. It's difficult to describe in words exactly how she looked,
but it was not an asexual pose in the sense that the audience
could forget that she was an attractive woman. She was dressed
in a loose-fitting, silky white blouse, a softly gathered skirt and
boots—not a "sexy" outfit, but one that made no attempt to
deny the fact that she was a woman. But when she spoke about
the balanced person, she was just there—a person with no
apologies about being a woman and with no intention of ex-
ploiting the fact that she was a woman. Her nonverbal communication said exactly what her words did, about being simply a person, instead of a "masculine" or "feminine" person.

Elsa summed up what this chapter is all about.

Suggested reading: Nancy M. Henley, *Body Politics* (Englewood Cliffs, N.J.: Prentice-Hall, 1977).

12

As Others See You

Evaluating and Improving
Your Spoken Image

How often have people come up to you after a speech and said, "That sure was boring. Sure was hard to stay awake through that one," or, "Sure made a mess of that one, didn't you?"?

Never.

People shake your hand, smile, and tell you how much they enjoyed it, whether they mean it or not. The higher your position, the fewer people dare criticize you in any way. This includes an honest appraisal of your speaking abilities. It's a rare employee who will risk telling his boss he's a lousy speaker.

So how do you evaluate your spoken image? How do you get honest feedback from other people? How can you find out how others really see you and hear you?

The Videotape

Seeing yourself on videotape is the most effective way I know to get outside yourself and see yourself as others see you. Obviously you're not going to have access to videotape equipment every time you make a speech, but if ever it is possible, have a speech videotaped. If you are considering enrolling in a speaking course, try to find one that uses videotape. It's by far the fastest, most efficient and most effective way to size up your speaking strengths and weaknesses.

There is no feedback more total or more objective than videotape because first, it reproduces your total image, both visual and aural; and second, it lets you see for yourself. If a friend or a colleague tells you you are a good speaker, you may not respect their judgment, you may think they're being nice rather than honest, or you may think they're biased in your favor. Bruce, the pharmaceutical salesman described in Chapter 4, simply couldn't believe it when people told him he was a good speaker because an unpleasant high school speaking experience had convinced him he would never be able to speak well. Seeing himself on videotape was a revelation to him: He saw for himself how good he was. Another person could never have convinced him of it.

By the same token, if someone tells you your voice is too high, that you slouch, or that you need to loosen up your body, you may not be convinced. A videotape has the inherent reassurance of a machine: It has no ulterior motive and it lets you see it like it is.

People play all kinds of tricks on themselves to deceive themselves about the kind of image they project. I have had people with protruding teeth, squeaky voices and even pronounced stutters who have said to me in surprise, "Oh, do my teeth stick out?" "Is my voice high?" "Do I stutter?" In Chapter

11 I described the discrepancy between the image many men and women project and the way they see themselves. Many had no conception of the gap between the two until they saw themselves on videotape.

I am constantly amazed at people's reactions when they see themselves on videotape. Time and again, it's as if they were seeing and hearing themselves for the first time. They really see the extra twenty pounds they've been lugging for ten years; they see the stiff way they stand; they hear the lack of energy in their voices, the *um*'s, the *you see*'s, the *you know*'s.

Becoming aware of the kind of image you project is the first step toward controlling it or altering it. I have what many people would call a wild hairdo: naturally curly, very thick, auburn hair worn *au naturel*. My hair, combined with my dress, the way I move, and my energetic voice, all label me as a strong, possibly aggressive, woman. I am aware that I project this kind of image. I do not change who I am, but I balance it by being especially careful to be sensitive to the feelings of people I come in contact with.

Videotape is devastatingly honest—too much so for some people. Sarah, an account executive working for a public relations agency, had deluded herself into thinking she was an attractive, assertive woman. On videotape, she saw a mousy, overweight woman with a high, squeaky voice. She was so shaken by what she saw that tears filled her eyes. When I asked her what she thought of her spoken image, she was unable to say anything more than a choked "I don't like it." Over the years, she had built a totally distorted self-image as a defense mechanism. She couldn't face the reality about herself: She couldn't admit she was fat, and she heard her voice at least an octave lower than it really was. After the initial shock of seeing herself on videotape, Sarah withdrew into herself. She attended the rest of the seminar, but remained emotionally detached and made no real effort to improve her speaking abilities. Because she couldn't face the truth about herself, she was incapable of even approaching the second step, taking the risk of changing her spoken image.

The Tape Recorder

A tape recorder cannot tell you how you look, but it can give you an objective reading of how you sound. As I mentioned in the chapter on voice, many people don't recognize their voice when they hear it on tape the first time—further evidence of how out of touch many people are with their spoken image. When we speak, we do hear our voice slightly differently than others do, but the difference is small. The real reason many people don't recognize their voice on tape, or else think it is distorted, is because they don't listen to their voice. They hear what they want to hear—like Sarah, who heard her voice much lower than it really was.

Like videotape, a tape recorder doesn't embellish or alter the sound of your voice or your speech patterns one iota. It merely reproduces them—hesitations, fillers, inconsistencies and all. A tape recorder is the most practical tool you can acquire to improve your spoken image, because it is inexpensive, portable and easily used. As I said in Chapter 9, a speech by definition is spoken, so you should practice it by talking it. Use a tape recorder first to organize your ideas, then to practice delivering your speech over and over again. There is no better way to hear yourself objectively than on tape.

Improving your spoken image doesn't mean just learning how to give a speech better. It means learning to speak more effectively in every speaking situation. So I suggest using a tape recorder for much more than dry runs for speeches. If your job involves repeatedly being asked similar questions, practice answering them on tape. If you have a point of view you particularly want to get across, practice slipping it into your answers. This kind of practice is especially important for salesmen who must deal with customers' questions and objections, and representatives of organizations.

Set a tape recorder next to your telephone and press the start button every time you talk on the telephone for a week or two. Then sit down and play it back all at once. Listen—really listen—to the sound of your voice, the clarity of your articulation, and for upward inflection, nervous laughter, fillers, inarticulate expression of your ideas, too low or too high an energy level.

Carry a tape recorder in your car, especially if you spend a lot of time in it. Practice speeches; concoct imaginary conversations between you and your boss, you and a colleague, you and a friend. Experiment with your voice: If you feel it is too high, too low, or not strong enough, take it to the limit in the opposite direction. Let yourself go; you're all alone. The only risk you're taking is an occasional baffled look from the driver of an adjacent car.

Remember, your voice tells who you are.

The Mirror: Too Subjective

A mirror is useful for checking details of your visual image, such as whether your slip is showing, your tie is straight, or your jacket fits. It is also helpful in working on posture. But a mirror is not an effective way to check your overall visual image—because it is too subjective. And it is virtually useless for checking your spoken image.

When we look at ourselves in a mirror we see what we want to see. We do magic things with our eyes, we smile, we move so that we see ourselves at our most flattering angle.

Watching yourself in a mirror also contradicts a basic tenet of speaking—reaching out to your audience. When you use a mirror, you focus on yourself rather than on your audience. It is next to impossible to relax and let go when you are watching yourself perform.

Photographs

Photographs are much more useful to check your visual image. How often have you seen a photograph and said, "Oh, that doesn't look like me," or, "That's a terrible picture of me"? Photographs do not always show you at your best, but a camera doesn't lie any more than a videotape or a tape recorder. The person you see in a photograph may not be you at your most attractive, but it is a you that other people sometimes see. If the reality spotlighted by a photograph is harsh, try to learn from it. There is truth in every photograph, even if it is only partial. Make a list of adjectives that describe the visual image you see in the photograph. Then list the changes you would like to see.

Questionnaires

If you really want to know what your audience thinks of your speech, don't rely on spontaneous, verbal comments after it is over. When you finish speaking, tell the audience that you are trying to improve your speaking abilities and would like their honest appraisal. Then pass around a questionnaire, emphasizing that you don't want empty praise; you want constructive criticism. Tell them there is no need to sign their names.

This is not an easy thing to do, especially if you are unsure of yourself as a speaker. It involves risk, because you may get negative feedback. But if you're serious about finding out the truth about your spoken image, this is an effective way to do so. If you emphasize that you don't want insincere pats on the back, and if the questionnaires are anonymous, you will get some useful, honest feedback. Use the questionnaire that follows as a model if you wish.

SPEECH EVALUATION

(a suggested format)

Content

1. State briefly the most useful information in the speech.
2. State briefly the least useful information in the speech.
3. The information was
   a. too simple
   b. too complicated
   c. appropriate
4. (If appropriate): What did you gain personally from the speech?
5. Additional comments about the content of the speech:

Delivery

1. The speaker appeared comfortable with the material.
   yes   no
2. The speaker projected
   a. warmth   yes   no
   b. energy   yes   no
   c. authority   yes   no
   d. sensitivity to   yes   no
      audience
   e. good eye contact   yes   no
   f. relaxed body   yes   no
   (This list can vary according to what you want to know and how specific you want to be.)
3. Additional comments:

Group Practice

You may find you need the structure and incentive of a group to really make strides improving your spoken image. The least expensive way is to form a group of colleagues or friends, all of whom are interested in becoming more effective speakers. Even meeting with one other person can be helpful if you both are seriously motivated.

I suggest that every person in the group read this book before meeting the first time. Then, working from my principles, you can take turns speaking and critiquing one another. Beware of the danger of giving only positive feedback. To make changes you must increase your self-awareness. A group can do this only if everyone in it is devastatingly honest.

If you decide on professional help, investigate courses offered in your community, bearing in mind the following guidelines: Don't even consider enrolling in a course unless the teacher has a reputation as an excellent speaker. A battery of degrees is meaningless if he cannot speak well. Be sure the course emphasizes performance rather than written work, history of rhetoric, or some other academic approach. And don't go near a course that takes a formal approach to speaking and tries to pour you into a polished, perfect mold. Also, be sure the group is not too large. I limit my seminars to ten persons because when there are any more than that, people cannot get the individual attention they need to increase self-awareness and make changes.

Taking Risks

I hope I have made it clear by now that becoming an effective speaker doesn't mean learning to do phony things with your voice or body or changing into a different person. It should bring out the best in you, or to phrase it another way, allow you to become the best of you. Nevertheless, changing ingrained habits is never easy and always involves personal risk. I like to compare improving your spoken image to acquiring a new sports skill. The first time you hold a tennis racket or golf club it feels strange and uncomfortable, but in time, as you master the skill, it becomes comfortable and feels natural.

We begin building our spoken image the moment we let out our first sound. By the time we reach adulthood our spoken image involves patterns and habits as ingrained as our eating habits. When a child stops crawling and starts walking he abandons an established habit in favor of an entirely new one that works better. It's not nearly so easy for an adult to abandon an old pattern for a new one, even if he knows the new one will be more effective.

We are creatures of habit, and change rarely comes easily. It is physically and mentally taxing to discard old patterns and adopt new ones, and there is an emotional dimension as well. People who know us are used to a certain kind of behavior from us. When we change, they may not like it; they may laugh at it; or they may feel threatened by it because they don't know what to expect from us any more. Change involves personal risk. If a person decides his articulation is sloppy and starts enunciating more clearly, his colleagues or friends may ridicule him for trying to assume airs. A woman who cuts her hair and starts wearing jackets instead of sweaters because she wants to project a more professional image must be prepared to give up the paternalistic or protective treatment that traditional "femininity" inspires. A rigidly controlled man who begins moving and gesturing more freely and putting more energy into his voice runs the risk of being considered loose or unprofessional by some people.

How fast you make changes and how much you change

depends on you—on how conservative you are by nature, on how many changes you feel you need to make, and on how motivated you are. Make changes gradually, as you feel comfortable with them. Test yourself in nonthreatening situations to build up your self-confidence. Working alone with your tape recorder is a good way to start. Your tape recorder can't talk back to you and it can't laugh at you. An informal group of people all interested in improving their speaking skills is another excellent place to test changes. I encourage my students to risk as much as possible in the controlled, receptive environment of the seminar. If they push themselves to their limit there, they will find it that much easier to make less drastic changes when they are in a more critical atmosphere.

How open people are to taking risks varies widely. Sean, the crash investigator described in Chapter 11, took the risk of drastically lowering his energy level, although he had built his career on a super-energetic style. At the other extreme is a person like Sarah, who couldn't even face herself as she was, let alone risk making any changes.

Most of us are somewhere in between. Eric is a good example of a middle-of-the-road person. Eric wasn't a bad speaker but he had an annoying habit of squinting and wrinkling his nose and forehead. He wore gray-tinted glasses that made it difficult to see his eyes when he talked, so I suggested he take them off. When he did so, the change was instantaneous and dramatic. Not only could you see his eyes clearly, but all his irritating facial contortions vanished. They had all been caused by his glasses, which didn't fit him and kept falling down onto his nose. When his face relaxed and you could see his eyes, he instantly became much more open.

But even when he saw the transformation on videotape, Eric still wasn't convinced his glasses had to go. I told him that becoming an effective speaker involved being willing to reach out, and that if he wasn't willing to make a simple physical change such as getting contact lenses or buying glasses with clear lenses that were comfortable on his face, he was wasting his time at the seminar. Reluctantly, he discarded his old glasses—and took the first step toward becoming a more effective speaker.

You know what involves the most risk for you personally. Maybe it's speaking without notes, maybe it's holding a silence, maybe it's moving away from the lectern. Whatever it is, try it; test it in a noncritical situation where it really doesn't matter if your mind goes blank for a moment or you fumble-mumble or trip over the microphone cord. Test new speaking methods on people you don't feel self-conscious with or whom you know will be receptive. Sometimes it's easier to try a new style in front of people you don't know, who don't have preconceived ideas of you and your speaking style and will be less likely to question them.

And remember, anything is easier to do the second time, easier again the third time. Be kind to yourself and try it first when it won't be a disaster if you flub it.

Trying a New Way

It's always easier to take risks in a controlled situation. Part of the excitement of my seminars is seeing people begin with small risks, then risk more and more. The spirit is catching: As others in the group see one person taking the risk of trying a new way, they venture out as well.

If you practice speaking in a group situation, be supportive of one another but be honest too. Try role-playing, to encourage one another to make drastic changes. If you take three steps in a controlled situation, you may have the courage to take one or two when you're faced with a "real" audience.

13

The Best
You Can Be

According to *The Book of Lists*,* public speaking is the number-one fear of Americans, ahead of death, flying and loneliness. Yet more and more people are speaking in public. An estimated 100,000 meetings per week featuring speakers are held in this country.

We fear most what we do not understand—the unfamiliar, the new, the untested. I hope this book has broadened your understanding of what speaking should and can be. That's the first step toward conquering fear.

My main purpose in writing has been to broaden your understanding and increase your awareness—of what effective speaking means, of what kinds of goals you should set for yourself when you speak, and of yourself. Increasing your self-

* David Wallechinsky, Irving Wallace and Amy Wallace (New York: Wm. Morrow, 1977).

awareness is the most important part of the process. Learning to speak effectively does not mean just brushing up your articulation, improving your voice, learning how to use a lectern or organize a speech—although all these things can be part of it. Becoming an effective speaker does not mean improving isolated speaking skills. It involves the whole you. It means taking a long, hard look at the way you see yourself and the way others see you—at your self-image, your visual image and your spoken image.

I hope this book has helped you do that—develop a more objective awareness of yourself and how you appear to others. Because this is essential to becoming an effective speaker.

The Best You Can Be

Answer the questionnaire at the end of this chapter. Give each question careful thought. Then compare your answers with those you gave on the questionnaire at the beginning of the book. This should help you measure how much the book has helped you broaden your awareness.

The questionnaire at the end of this chapter can help you set long-term goals for yourself—but don't expect to achieve them immediately. Your goal today should be to be the best you can today, no more, no less. Two months from now, if you follow the guidelines in the book and keep working at it, you will be closer to your long-term goal.

You'll know when you're getting better. The signs are unmistakable. Your audiences will tell you. But even if they didn't, you'd know. Your growing sense of self-confidence will tell you. You will feel more in control of yourself and your life because you will be gaining control over a very important part of yourself—your spoken image.

The rewards of effective speaking go far beyond the po-

	Image I Project	Image I Would Like to Project	What I Can Do to Change My Image
1. My Spoken Image:	(e.g.) too authoritative	softer, more sensitive	work on audience awareness
2. My Visual Image:	(e.g.) too casual	more businesslike	more tailored clothing
3. My Voice:	(e.g.) lacks resonance	more depth, resonance, volume, authority	work on voice exercises
4. My Body: How relaxed I am; my posture; how I move	(e.g.) inhibited in movement, gestures	more relaxed, easygoing	work on relaxation exercises; practice gesturing more freely
5. My Nonverbal Behavior:	(e.g.) not enough eye contact; detached from audience	warmer, more involved with my audience	work on "reaching out," developing better eye contact

dium. You will be more comfortable with yourself and with other people in every situation. The sense of accomplishment, the feeling of power and self-confidence, the glow—these are things I cannot describe in words. You will only begin to appreciate what I mean when you experience it.

When you begin to really enjoy speaking, you'll experience a unique, delicious sense of power as well as human contact.

That's when you'll be moved to say: "I gave a speech last night and I wasn't good.

"No, I wasn't good . . . I was fantastic!"

Toward Effective Speaking

Now that you have read the book, answer the following questions:

1. List the qualities of an effective speaker.
2. Which do you possess?
3. Which can you develop? How?
4. How have your ideas about effective speaking changed since reading this book?
5. Set your own speaking goals by filling in the chart on page 216.

Appendix

Q.: I'm very nervous when I give a speech. What can I do about it?

A.: It is important to understand that no one can give you a magic cure-all that will guarantee you will never feel nervous again when you speak. There is no way to get rid of stress completely, but you can learn to understand it, control it, and make it work for you.

Nervousness affects you both mentally and physically. You can control nervousness mentally by carefully planning and rehearsing your opening, establishing eye contact with as many people as possible in the audience, and remembering that any audience is just people, most of whom want you to be comfortable.

But physical control of nervousness is also important. You can gain physical control by learning special breathing techniques. The most important aspect of breathing for relaxation is focusing on the exhale. Breathing for relaxation is outlined in Chapter 5.

Q.: Should I memorize my speech?

A.: No. Practice a speech to become thoroughly familiar with the ideas. Never memorize it word for word. If you memorize a speech, you will sacrifice spontaneity and contact with your audience because you will be using your energy to recall exact words rather than to reach out to your audience and watch their response.

Q.: Is it ever all right to use a manuscript speech?

A.: A manuscript speech sets up a barrier between you and your audience because it interferes with the natural rhythms of speech, makes it difficult to establish eye contact with your audience, and prevents your personality from coming through.

I usually don't recommend a manuscript speech. However, I concede that there are times when a manuscript speech is almost obligatory, such as when a corporation wants representatives in several offices to deliver the same speech.

When you must deliver a manuscript speech, edit it so that it reads the way *you* would say it, not the way someone else wrote it. Mark it for pauses, not emphasis. Practice it as you would any speech—to become familiar with the ideas rather than the specific words. Try to get away from the words on the page as often as possible, to establish eye contact with your audience and develop rapport with them.

Q.: How can I make my audience listen to me?

A.: You cannot take it for granted that any audience is going to listen. Every audience is tacitly asking the question "Why should I bother to listen?"

You must give your audience a reason to listen in the first few minutes of your talk. How you open your speech is crucial for pulling your audience in. Chapter 9 gives specific suggestions on openings that "hook" an audience.

Talk in big ideas that are easily and quickly grasped by ear. Tailor your material to your audience: Tell them why it is important to them personally. Humanize it by using concrete examples that the audience can relate to.

Asking an audience to listen—really listen—is asking them to exert a lot of energy. So you have to give out a lot of energy to keep them listening.

Q.: How can I deal with a hostile audience?

A.: Active listening—satisfying the hostile person(s) that you understand why he feels the way he does, that you don't feel personally hostile toward him, and that you want to establish common ground with him—is the most effective way to deal with hostility and to keep yourself from becoming emotionally involved. Active listening is described in detail in Chapter 7 but, briefly, it means listening for the meaning behind the words a person uses, not just to the words themselves.

Q.: When I talk for a long time my throat gets sore. What can I do about it?

A.: There is no sixty-second answer. If you use your voice a lot, you must learn to use it properly. This is going to take daily time and effort; it will not happen overnight.

Relaxation and proper breathing are the basis of good voice production. If you use your voice constantly, however, you probably will have to do voice exercises. Chapter 6 details voice exercises to teach you to use your voice properly.

Q.: How should I behave on the speaking platform? How much should I move? How freely should I gesture?

A.: Your platform behavior should be as natural, as relaxed, as conversational and as real as it can be. It should never be described as formal, artificial or studied.

Stand in a balanced position with your feet apart (lined up under your armpits) to give your body stable support. Move as often as feels comfortable. Movement and gestures should not be preplanned; they should happen naturally. If you do not suppress your physical energy, you will move and gesture naturally, when it is appropriate to what you are saying.

Q.: Should I ask for group participation? If so, why?

A.: Genuine communication is always two-way, and it is difficult to be sure what your audience is thinking unless you invite their participation. You can do this through question-and-answer sessions or group discussions.

Also, people can listen quietly only for a limited length of time. They will tune out eventually if they are not asked to interact with the speaker in some way.

Q.: How should I dress when I give a speech?

A.: Comfort is important: Choose clothes that will enable you to move freely. Wear clothes you feel you look good in; this will bolster your self-confidence.

Don't adapt your dress to reflect what you think the audience will be wearing. Your clothes should project you, not mirror your audience.

Avoid anything that distracts from what you are saying— such as noisy or flashy jewelry, startling colors or excessively revealing clothes.

Q.: How long will it take me to become an effective speaker?
A.: Learning to speak effectively is a skill that must be learned. How long it takes is a very individual matter. It may take you a week or a year to become the speaker you want to be. How long it takes depends on many factors: how much you have to learn—and unlearn—how motivated you are, and how much time and effort you are willing to invest.

Becoming an effective speaker is not comparable to learning to ride a bicycle: If you don't continue to use and practice your speaking skills, you can lose them.

Thank You's

To Loral Dean, a versatile writer and good listener, who pulled it all together.

To Caroline Harkleroad, who helped make it happen, always in a good-natured, professional way.

To Frank Wiedemann, who contributed much to the chapter on relaxation, who has helped many Speakeasy students use their bodies more effectively, and who taught me to deal with stress in a more relaxed way.

To the business people, especially those in Atlanta, who have helped me and my business to grow.

To the friends who had time to listen.

To the students who were willing to risk.

About the Author

Sandy Linver is the President and founder of Speakeasy Inc., a consulting firm with offices in Atlanta and San Francisco. Nationally recognized as an expert on speaking, Linver travels throughout the United States working with top executives on their communication skills, conducting seminars, and speaking at conventions and meetings.

Linver's educational background includes degrees in speech arts and education, a master's degree in telecommunications, and teaching experience at the university level. Her professional experience includes eight years as a television interviewer and performer, with four years on a daily CBC network show in Canada.